한자를 알면 한국어가 쉬워진다
YOUR FIRST HANJA GUIDE

WRITTEN BY
TALK TO ME IN KOREAN
KONG & PARK

YOUR FIRST HANJA GUIDE

Learn Essential Chinese Characters Used in the Korean Language

Written by	TalkToMeInKorean and KONG & PARK
Edited by	Kyung-hwa Sun, Stephanie Bates, Emily Przylucki
Designed by	Yoona Sun
Voice Recording by	TalkToMeInKorean
Published by	KONG & PARK USA, Inc.
	1480 Renaissance Drive, Suite 412,
	Park Ridge, IL 60068 USA
	Tel +1 (847) 241 4845
	Fax +1 (312) 757 5553
	usaoffice@kongnpark.com
	www.kongnpark.com

Copyright © 2018 by TalkToMeInKorean and KONG & PARK, INC.

All rights reserved. No part of this book may be reproduced, stored in a retrieval system, or transmitted in any form or by any means (electronic, mechanical, photocopied, recorded or otherwise), without the prior written permission of the copyright holder.

1st published September 29, 2017
ISBN 978-1-63519-008-3
Library of Congress Control Number: 2017955510

DISTRIBUTORS

United States: KONG & PARK USA, Inc.
475 North Martingale Road, Suite 710
Schaumburg, IL 60173
Tel +1 (847) 241 4845
Fax +1 (312) 757 5553
usaoffice@kongnpark.com

United Kingdom and Europe: Kodansha Europe Ltd.
40 Stockwell Street
Greenwich, London SE10 8EY
Tel +44 (0)20-8293-0111
Fax +44 (0)20-8293-5533
info@kodansha.eu

Canada: Fitzhenry & Whiteside Ltd.
195 Allstate Parkway
Markham, Ontario L3R 4T8
Tel +1 (800) 387 9776
Fax +1 (800) 260 9777
bookinfo@fitzhenry.ca

Other countries: KONG & PARK, Inc.
85, Gwangnaru-ro 56-gil, Prime center 1518
Gwangjin-gu, Seoul, 05116 Korea
Tel +82 (0)2 565 1537
Fax +82 (0)2 3445 1080
info@kongnpark.com

Printed in Korea

한자를 알면
한국어가 쉬워진다

YOUR FIRST HANJA GUIDE

Learn Essential Chinese Characters
Used in the Korean Language

Table of Contents

Preface				11
How to Use This Book				12
People	Person			14
		person	人/亻	16
		enter	入	18
		make	作	20
		substitute / historical period	代	22
		year	年	24
		Review Quiz		26
		Flow Chart		27
		earlier	先	28
		light	光	30
		color	色	32
		fish	魚	34
		Review Quiz		36
		Flow Chart		37
		change	化	38
		flower	花	40
		north	北	42
		old	老	44
		long / elder	長	46
		die	死	48
		Review Quiz		50
		Flow Chart		51
		child / suffix	子	52
		study	學	54
		teach	敎	56
		woman	女	58

good	好	60
necessary / essential	要	62
mother	母	64
Review Quiz		66
Flow Chart		67

Body

68

body	身	70
big	大	72
beautiful	美	74
character / script	文	76
oneself	自	78
Review Quiz		80
Flow Chart		81
pain / pungent	辛	82
intimate / parent	親	84
new	新	86
meaning	意	88
Review Quiz		90
Flow Chart		91
mouth	口	92
name	名	94
article / object	品	96
add	加	98
country / nation	國	100
the people / subjects	民	102
Review Quiz		104
Flow Chart		105
old	古	106

	high	高	108
	center	中	110
	bear (fruit) / tie	結	112
	Review Quiz		114
	Flow Chart		115
	mind / heart	心/忄	116
	must / without fail	必	118
	nature	性	120
	love	愛	122
	feeling	情	124
	Review Quiz		126
	Flow Chart		127
	Hanja Sadaritagi (Ghost leg) Game		128
Hand			130
	hand	手	132
	father	父	134
	time	時	136
	special	特	138
	Review Quiz		140
	Flow Chart		141
	right	右	142
	left	左	144
	have / exist	有	146
	opposite	反	148
	Review Quiz		150
	Flow Chart		151
Foot			152
	foot	足	154

		go out	出	156
		right / correct	正	158
		subject	題	160
		Review Quiz		162
		Flow Chart		163
		summer	夏	164
		back / after	後	166
		winter	冬	168
		Review Quiz		170
		Flow Chart		171
		go	行	172
		move / transfer	運	174
		way / morals	道	176
		pass through	通	178
		Review Quiz		180
		Flow Chart		181
Life	Shelter			182
		house / -ist	家	184
		peaceful	安	186
		room	室	188
		Review Quiz		190
		Flow Chart		191
		door / gate	門	192
		ask	問	194
		interval / between	間	196
		Review Quiz		198
		Flow Chart		199
		inside	內	200

Learn Essential Chinese Characters Used in the Korean Language

		south	南	202
		city / market	市	204
		rain	雨	206
		Review Quiz		208
		Flow Chart		209
		Hanja Yut-Nori		210
	Tools			212
		fire	火	214
		autumn / fall	秋	216
		nothingness	無	218
		dot / spot	點	220
		Review Quiz		222
		Flow Chart		223
		power	力	224
		man	男	226
		move	動	228
		Review Quiz		230
		Flow Chart		231
		eat / food	食	232
		gather	會	234
		metal / gold	金	236
		Review Quiz		238
		Flow Chart		239
Nature	Animals			240
		cow	牛	242
		half	半	244
		divide / minute	分	246
		public	公	248

	truth	眞	250
	Review Quiz		252
	Flow Chart		253
Natural Scenery			254
	tree	木	256
	east	東	258
	west	西	260
	heavy	重	262
	cart / car	車	264
	Review Quiz		266
	Flow Chart		267
	school	校	268
	come	來	270
	music / pleasure	樂	272
	taste	味	274
	Review Quiz		276
	Flow Chart		277
	mountain	山	278
	world / lifetime	世	280
	tea	茶	282
	be born / life	生	284
	Review Quiz		286
	Flow Chart		287
Heavenly Bodies			288
	day / sun	日	290
	spring	春	292
	moon / month	月	294
	bright / next	明	296

a lot of / many		多	298
front		前	300
Review Quiz			302
Flow Chart			303
soil		土	304
land		地	306
place		場	308
Review Quiz			310
Flow Chart			311

Miscellaneous — 312

small		小	314
work		事	316
water		水	318
alcoholic drinks		酒	320
Review Quiz			322
Flow Chart			323
up		上	324
down		下	326
Review Quiz			328
Flow Chart			329
Hanja Board Game			330

Index — 332

Preface

"Do Korean people really know all of those Chinese characters?"

While walking down the street in Korea, you may see many sign boards that are written with Chinese characters. While watching some Korean television shows, you might also notice that they use Chinese characters in the subtitles. Perhaps you think, "Do all Koreans know so many characters?" or "How often are those characters actually used?"

If you have ever wondered this, then this book is for you! This book is also for anyone who wants to improve their Korean vocabulary as well as their general understanding of the Korean language, as thousands of Korean words used in daily conversation are based on Chinese characters, called Hanja in Korean.

This book contains essential Hanja characters that can be understood by most Korean adults and/or are commonly used on signs and in advertisements. For example, characters like 大 (big), 中 (medium), and 小 (small) are frequently used on restaurant menus to refer to dish portions, so they are easily recognized by almost anyone.

Learning and understanding Hanja will not only help you read words that are actually written in Chinese characters, but also help you expand your Korean vocabulary because they work as building blocks for many other words. It's similar to learning Latin-based suffixes or root words to expand your English vocabulary. You can achieve a similar result by learning Hanja. After studying with this book, you will even find yourself understanding difficult and formal words that were not even introduced in this book! Enjoy learning Hanja!

How to Use This Book

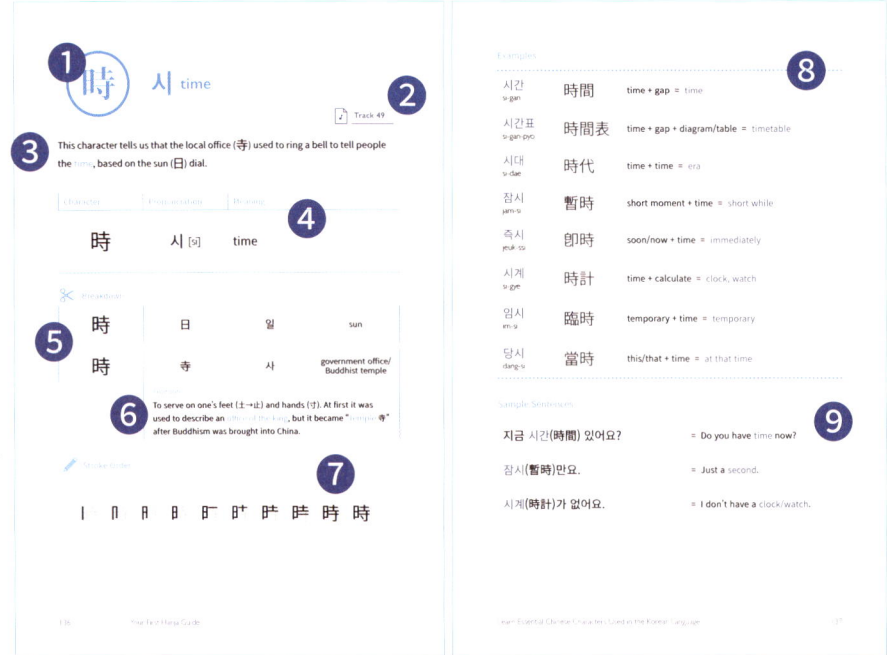

1. Section title
2. Audio track number that corresponds to the section. You can listen to the pronunciation of the character, examples, and sample sentences.
3. Etymology of the character. This helps you better understand the origin and meaning of the character for easier memorization.
4. Korean pronunciation and meaning of the Chinese character.
5. Breakdown of the Chinese character. All Chinese characters are composed of a few base characters except for radicals (base characters). This section introduces the Korean pronunciation and meaning of each part. If the main Chinese character is a radical, it doesn't have this "Breakdown" section.
6. Footnote/Sidenote. Additional explanation of the base characters introduced in the "Breakdown" section.

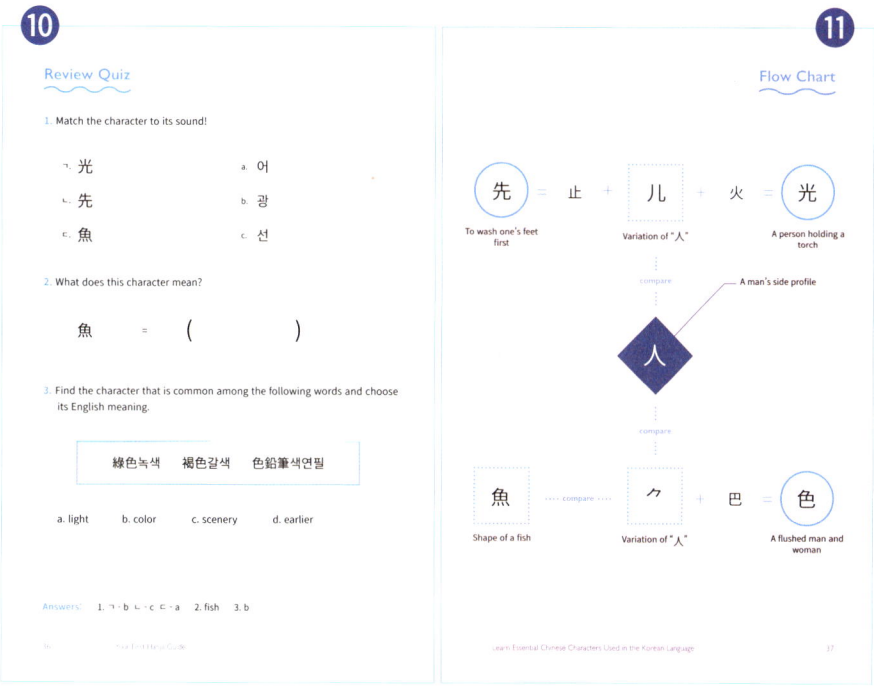

7. Stroke order of the main Chinese character. Practice writing it in your notebook.

8. Korean vocabulary words that include the main character. Sino-Korean words, which use Chinese characters, are relatively formal in general, so TalkToMeInKorean tried to pick ones that are widely used for this book.

9. Sample sentences that use Sino-Korean words. You can see how the Sino-Korean words from above can be used in a sentence.

10. Review quiz. After you finish learning 3-6 Chinese characters, you can test yourself with this quiz section.

11. Flow chart. Through this chart, you can see how the 3-6 Chinese characters that you just learned are related to each other. If you add (+) a certain character to the radical, or base character, it creates (=) a new word.

Person

學―教―女―好―要―母― 魚―化―花―北―老―長―死―子― 人―入―作―代―年―先―光―色―

 **인** person

🎵 Track 01

The side profile of a person. It means 'man.'

Character	Pronunciation	Meaning
人/亻	인 [in]	person, human

✏️ Stroke Order

Examples

개인 gae-in	個人	piece + person = individual
인물 in-mul	人物	person + object = person
인사 in-sa	人事	person + work = greeting
노인 no-in	老人	old + person = elderly, old person
인간 in-gan	人間	person + between = human
인구 in-gu	人口	person + mouth = population
인기 in-kki	人氣	person + energy = popularity
부인 bu-in	婦人	wife + person = wife
외국인 oe-gu-gin	外國人	outside + country + person = foreigner
주인 ju-in	主人	host + person = owner

Sample Sentences

저 가수는 인기(人氣)가 정말 많아요. = That singer is really popular.

제 부인(婦人)이랑 딸이에요. = This is my wife and my daughter.

저 사람이 이 집 주인(主人)이에요. = That person is the owner of this house.

 입 enter

 Track 02

The entrance to a cave or mud hut. It means 'to enter.'

Character	Pronunciation	Meaning
入	입 [ip]	enter

Sidenote

This character is a radical but no one is sure of the origin. Not to be confused with "person 人."

 Stroke Order

Examples

입구 ip-kku	入口	enter + mouth = entrance
입학 i-pak	入學	enter + learn/school = entering school, starting school
출입 chu-rip	出入	go out + enter = going in and out
수입 su-ip	收入	harvest + enter = income
신입생 si-nip-ssaeng	新入生	new + enter + person = new student, freshman, first year student
입원 i-bwon	入院	enter + house/public institution = being hospitalized
입사 ip-ssa	入社	enter + gather/company = joining a company
입장료 ip-jjang-lyo	入場料	enter + yard/place + count/fee = admission
입양 i-byang	入養	enter + raise/foster = adoption
입금 ip-kkeum	入金	enter + money = deposit

Sample Sentences

입구(入口)가 어디예요? = Where is the entrance?

어제 입학(入學)한 신입생이에요. = I am a freshman who entered school yesterday.

놀이 공원 입장료(入場料)가 얼마예요? = How much is admission to the amusement park?

 make

 Track 03

The character "乍", which signifies a person harvesting with tools, means "sudden"; by adding the subject person (亻) it reinforces the meaning of to do.

Character	Pronunciation	Meaning
作	작 [jak]	make, do

✂ Breakdown

作	人/亻	인	person
作	乍	사/작	suddenly/occur

✏ Stroke Order

作 作 作 作 作 作 作

Examples

시작 si-jak	始作	first + make/do = start
작가 jak-kka	作家	make + house/person = author
작품 jak-pum	作品	make + stuff/product = work of art
제작 je-jak	製作	make + make = making, production
작업 ja-geop	作業	do + job = work
조작 jo-jak	造作	fake + make = fabrication
작문 jang-mun	作文	make + sentence = composition
작곡 jak-kkok	作曲	make + music = music composition, writing music
작사 jak-ssa	作詞	make + word/writing = writing lyrics
명작 myeong-jak	名作	name/reputation + make = masterpiece

Sample Sentences

수업을 시작(始作)할 거예요.   = We will start the class.

작사(作詞)는 누가 했어요?   = Who wrote the lyrics?

이 그림은 명작(名作)이에요.   = This painting is a masterpiece.

대 substitute / historical period

 Track 04

A person (亻) using a practice bow and arrow (弋) instead of a real one. Because a more recent era in history replaces a previous one, this character came to mean 'historical periods' as well.

Character	Pronunciation	Meaning
代	대 [dae]	substitute, historical period, time, era

✂ Breakdown

代	人/亻	인	person
代	弋	익	nocked arrow

✏ Stroke Order

代 代 代 代 代

Examples

대표 dae-pyo	代表	substitute + leader = representative
시대 si-dae	時代	time + era = historical period
세대 se-dae	世代	human + era = generation
교대 gyo-dae	交代	exchange + substitute = rotation, taking turns, shift
대리 dae-ri	代理	substitute + govern = deputy, proxy
대역 dae-yeok	代役	substitute + role/part = understudy, stand-in
십대 sip-ttae	十代	ten + era = teenage years
대신 dae-sin	代身	substitute + body/oneself = instead

Sample Sentences

저희 회사 대표(代表)님이에요.   = He is the president of our company.

교대(交代)로 운전해요.   = Let's take turns driving.

제가 대신(代身)할게요.   = I will do it instead.

 년 year

 Track 05

A man (人) carrying sheaves of rice (禾) reminds us of harvests. The Chinese harvest once a year, so this character means 'year.'

Character	Pronunciation	Meaning
年	년, 연	year

✂ Breakdown

年	𠂉→人	인	person
年	牛→禾	화	rice plant

Sidenote

Ancient Chinese texts show that this character is a combination of rice (禾) and a person (人).

✏ Stroke Order

Your First Hanja Guide

Examples

작년 jang-nyeon	昨年	yesterday/previous + year = last year
내년 nae-nyeon	來年	come + year = next year
매년 mae-nyeon	每年	always/every + year = every year
연말 yeon-mal	年末	year + last = the end of the year
학년 hang-nyeon	學年	learn/school + year = grade
소년 so-nyeon	少年	young + year = boy
신년 sin-nyeon	新年	new + year = new year
연하 yeo-na	年下	year + under/below = being younger than someone
중년 jung-nyeon	中年	middle + year = middle age

Sample Sentences

매년(每年) 하는 행사예요.   = It's an event that takes place every year.

연말(年末)에는 항상 바빠요.   = I am always busy around the end of the year.

지금 3학년(學年)이에요.   = I am in my third year of school now.

Review Quiz

1. Match the character to its sound!

ㄱ. 代   a. 인

ㄴ. 作   b. 대

ㄷ. 入   c. 입

ㄹ. 人   d. 작

2. What does this character mean?

人   =   (   )

3. Find the character that is common among the following words and choose its English meaning.

| 昨年작년   來年내년   每年매년   新年신년 |

a. year   b. make   c. enter   d. substitute / historical period

Answers: 1. ㄱ - b ㄴ - d ㄷ - c ㄹ - a   2. person   3. a

Flow Chart

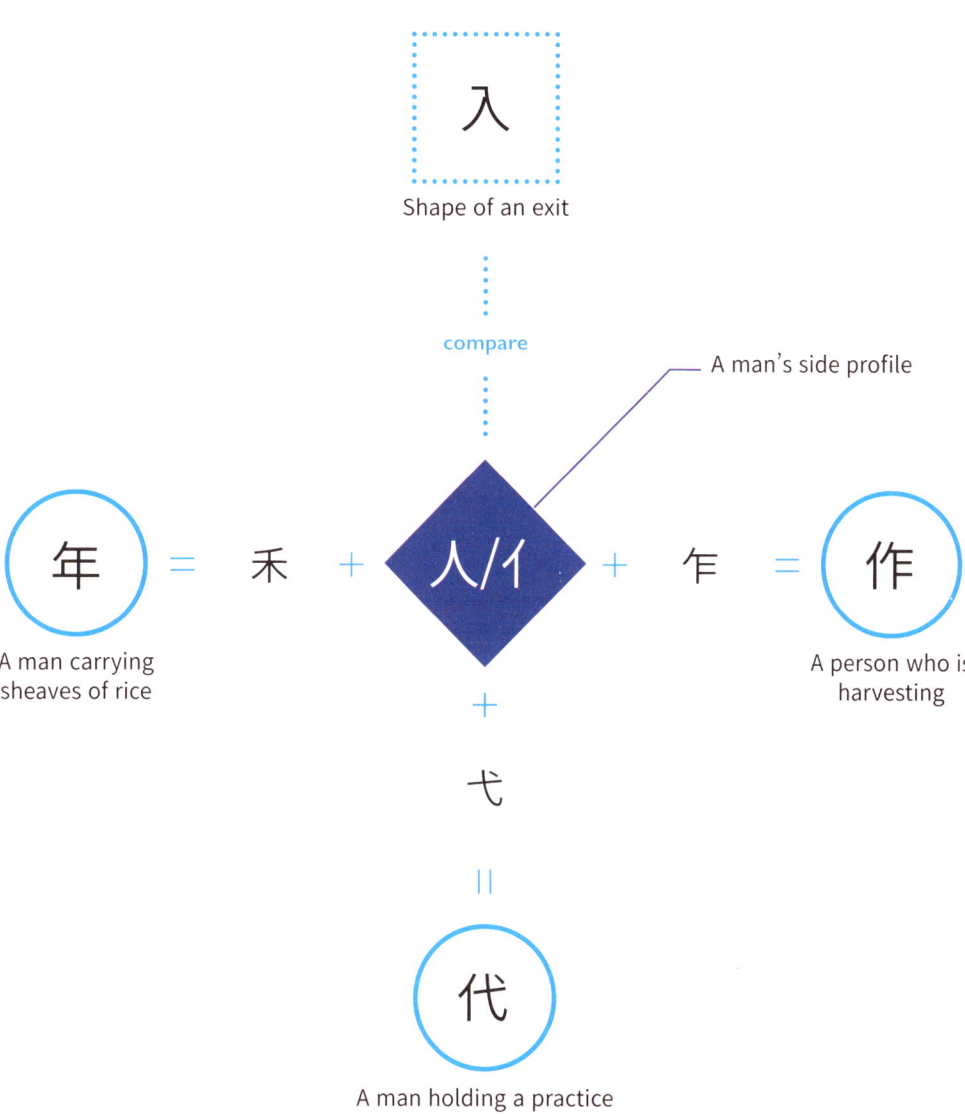

Learn Essential Chinese Characters Used in the Korean Language

선 **earlier**

 Track 06

Before entering a sacred place, a person (儿) must first wash his feet (止).

Character	Pronunciation	Meaning
先	선 [seon]	earlier, beforehand, first, lead

✂ **Breakdown**

先	生 → 止	지	foot/stop

Footnote
"止" represents the shape of a foot and means 'foot.'

先	儿	인	person

✏ **Stroke Order**

先 先 先 先 先 先

28 Your First Hanja Guide

Examples

우선 u-seon	優先	excellent + first = above all
선생 seon-saeng	先生	lead + person = teacher
선배 seon-bae	先輩	earlier + group/generation = older alumnus, more experienced person in the group
선약 seo-nyak	先約	earlier + arrange/promise = previous engagement
선착순 seon-chak-ssun	先着順	first + attach/arrive + order = first come, first served
선불 seon-bul	先拂	beforehand + pay = payment in advance, prepayment
선진국 seon-jin-guk	先進國	lead + advance + country = advanced country

Sample Sentences

저는 수학 선생(先生)님이에요.   = I am a mathematics teacher.

선약(先約)이 있어요.   = I have a previous engagement.

선착순(先着順) 100명.   = The first 100 people will be served.

광 light

 Track 07

This character represents a person (儿) holding a torch (火). It means 'light, sparkle, shine' from the image of a person holding up a torch and lighting the way.

Character	Pronunciation	Meaning
光	광 [gwang]	light, scenery

✂ Breakdown

光	𤇾 → 火	화	fire
光	儿	인	person

✏ Stroke Order

30 Your First Hanja Guide

Examples

| 관광
gwan-gwang | 觀光 | see + scenery = sightseeing |

| 관광지
gwan-gwang-ji | 觀光地 | see + scenery + ground/place = tourist spot |

| 야광
ya-gwang | 夜光 | night + light = glow-in-the-dark, luminous |

| 영광
yeong-gwang | 榮光 | honor + light = glory, honor |

| 후광
hu-gwang | 後光 | back + light = halo |

Sample Sentences

광화문은 관광(觀光)하기 좋아요. = Gwang-hwa-mun is good for sightseeing.

부산은 유명한 관광지(觀光地)예요. = Busan is a famous tourist spot.

야광(夜光) 별을 샀어요. = I bought some glow-in-the-dark stars.

 색 color

 Track 08

One person (⺈) on top of another (巴) making love. This character means 'color', because the couple are flushed.

Character	Pronunciation	Meaning
色	색 [saek]	color

 Breakdown

色	⺈→人	인	person
色	巴	파	person/hope

Footnote
"巴" represents a fat baby and means 'person.'

✏️ Stroke Order

Your First Hanja Guide

Examples

녹색 nok-ssaek	綠色	green + color = green
색연필 saeng-nyeon-pil	色鉛筆	color + lead + brush = colored pencil
갈색 gal-ssaek	褐色	brown + color = brown
염색 yeom-saek	染色	dye + color = dyeing
색맹 saeng-maeng	色盲	color + blind = color-blindness

Sample Sentences

저는 녹색(綠色)을 제일 좋아해요.   = I like the color green the most.

갈색(褐色)으로 염색(染色)했어요.   = I dyed my hair brown.

 어 fish

 Track 09

Head (㇗), body (田), and tail (灬) are combined together to form a fish.

Character	Pronunciation	Meaning
魚	어 [eo]	fish

✏️ Stroke Order

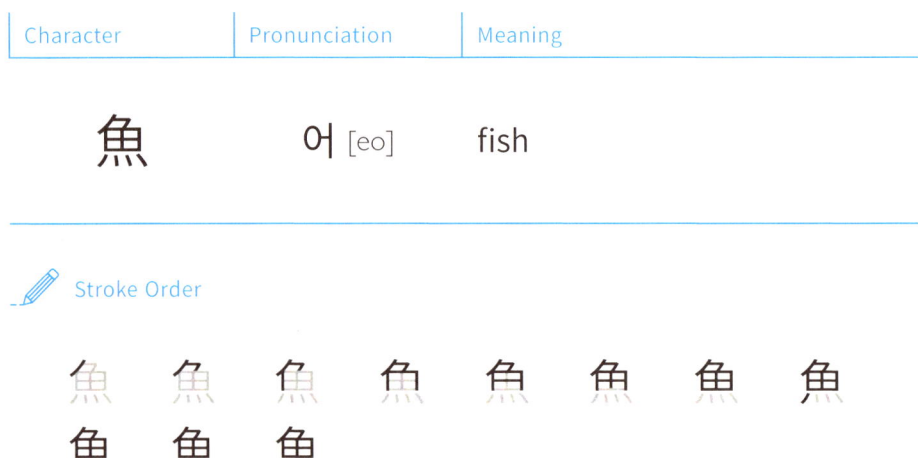

Examples

어류 eo-ryu	魚類	fish + group = fish, various kinds of fish
인어 i-neo	人魚	human + fish = mermaid
열대어 yeol-ttae-eo	熱帶魚	hot + belt + fish = tropical fish
악어 a-geo	鰐魚	crocodile + fish = crocodile, alligator

Sample Sentences

인어(人魚) 공주 이야기 알아요? = Do you know The Little Mermaid story?

열대어(熱帶魚)는 색깔이 정말 예뻐요. = Tropical fish have very pretty colors.

동물원에 악어(鰐魚)가 세 마리 있어요. = There are three crocodiles at the zoo.

Review Quiz

1. Match the character to its sound!

ㄱ. 光　　　　　　　　a. 어

ㄴ. 先　　　　　　　　b. 광

ㄷ. 魚　　　　　　　　c. 선

2. What does this character mean?

魚　=　(　　　　　)

3. Find the character that is common among the following words and choose its English meaning.

> 綠色녹색　　褐色갈색　　色鉛筆색연필

a. light　　b. color　　c. scenery　　d. earlier

Answers:　1. ㄱ - b ㄴ - c ㄷ - a　2. fish　3. b

Flow Chart

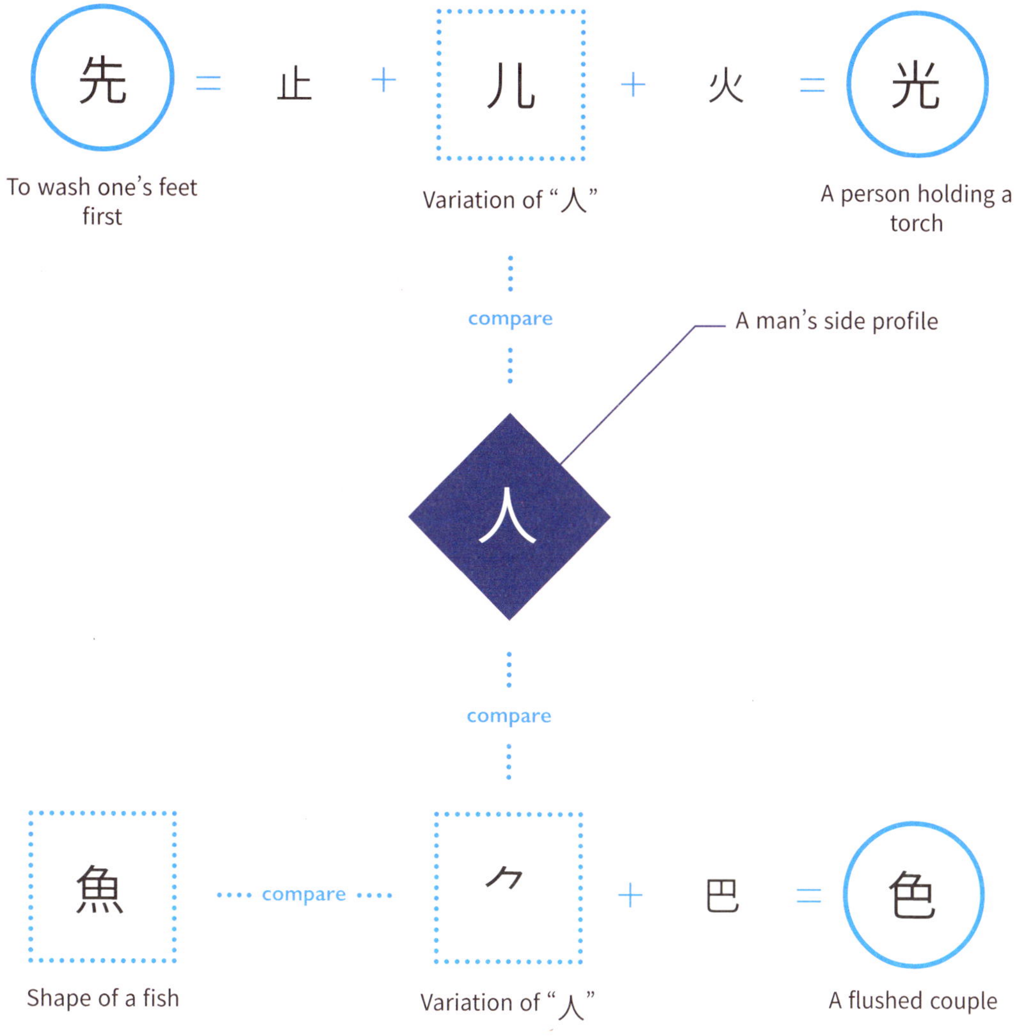

先 = 止 + 儿 + 火 = 光

To wash one's feet first　　　　Variation of "人"　　　　A person holding a torch

compare

A man's side profile

人

compare

魚 ····compare···· 勹 + 巴 = 色

Shape of a fish　　　　Variation of "人"　　　　A flushed couple

Learn Essential Chinese Characters Used in the Korean Language

 change

 Track 10

A man standing (亻) and a man upside down (匕). A person (亻) is born a baby but dies an old man (匕), which means everything changes.

Character	Pronunciation	Meaning
化	화 [hwa]	change, become

✂ Breakdown

化	人/亻	인	person
化	匕	비	person

Footnote
Ancient Chinese texts explain that because "匕" looks like a mirrored "person 人 [인]", it also means 'the elderly', a frail person.

✏ Stroke Order

化 化 化 化

Examples

변화 byeo-nwa	變化	change + change = change
문화 mu-nwa	文化	writing + change = culture
소화 so-hwa	消化	disappear + change = digestion
화장 hwa-jang	化粧	change + dress up/make up = makeup
화장품 hwa-jang-pum	化粧品	change + dress up/make up + stuff/product = cosmetics
화장실 hwa-jang-sil	化粧室	change + dress up/make up + house/room = bathroom, toilet
화학 hwa-hak	化學	change + learn = chemistry

Sample Sentences

소화(消化)가 잘 안돼요.   = I have bad digestion.

오늘 화장(化粧)을 안 했어요.   = I am not wearing makeup today.

화장실(化粧室)이 어디예요?   = Where is the bathroom?

 화 flower

 Track 11

As time goes by, a baby grows into an adult, just as plants (艹) change (化) into beautiful flowers.

Character	Pronunciation	Meaning
花	화 [hwa]	flower

✂ Breakdown

花	艹	초	grass
花	化	화	change

✏ Stroke Order

花 花 花 花 花 花 花 花

Examples

화분 花盆 flower + jar/pot = flowerpot
hwa-bun

생화 生花 live/be born + flower = natural flower, real flower
saeng-hwa

화단 花壇 flower + altar = flower bed
hwa-dan

국화 國花 country + flower = national flower
gu-kwa

Sample Sentences

꽃을 화분(花盆)에 심어요. = I plant flowers in a flowerpot.

학교 화단(花壇)에 꽃이 많아요. = There are many flowers in the school flower bed.

한국의 국화(國花)는 뭐예요? = What is the national flower of Korea?

 북 north

 Track 12

Two people (匕) standing facing away from each other means 'to turn one's back on.' People prefer to face the light and build houses facing south, so this character became 'north', the direction one faces when their back is turned to the south.

Character	Pronunciation	Meaning
北	북, 배 [buk, bae]	north, run away

Breakdown

| 北 | ㅓ → 匕 | 비 | person |
| 北 | 匕 | 비 | person |

Stroke Order

Examples

북극
buk-kkeuk

北極

north + devoted/peak = the North Pole

패배
pae-bae

敗北

lose + run away = defeat

Sample Sentences

북극(北極)에 가 봤어요?   = Have you been to the North Pole?

패배(敗北)의 이유가 뭐지?   = What is the reason for the defeat?

 노 old

 Track 13

"耂" cannot be used on its own, so the Chinese added the character for 'old (匕)' to stress its meaning.

Character	Pronunciation	Meaning
老	로, 노 [ro, no]	old

 Breakdown

老	耂	로	old
老	匕	비	person

Sidenote

"耂" is originally short for "old 老." The word "ancient" illustrates that an old man (耂) with a hunched back and long hair is holding onto his walking stick (匕).

Stroke Order

老 老 老 老 老 老

Examples

노인 no-in	老人	old + person = old person
노후 no-hu	老後	old + back/after = one's later years
노약자 no-yak-jja	老弱者	old + weak + person = the old and the infirm
노부부 no-bu-bu	老夫婦	old + husband + wife = old couple
노처녀 no-cheo-nyeo	老處女	old + virgin/unmarried woman = old unmarried woman, "old maid"
노총각 no-chong-gak	老總角	old + unmarried man = old bachelor
노인정 no-in-jeong	老人亭	old + person + pavilion = senior citizens' center
노안 no-an	老眼	old + eye = presbyopia, age-related farsightedness

Sample Sentences

지하철에는 노약자(老弱者)석이 있어요.
= On the subway, there is seating for the old and the infirm.

노후(老後)를 준비하세요.
= Prepare for your later years.

노처녀(老處女)와 노총각(老總角)이 만나서 결혼했어요.
= An old unmarried woman and an old unmarried man met and got married.

 長 **장** long / elder

 Track 14

Like "old 老", this character also represents an old man with long hair and a stick. But whereas "老" came to mean 'old', "長" became 'long.'

Character	Pronunciation	Meaning
長	장 [jang]	long, elder, better, adult, leader

 Stroke Order

Examples

회장 hoe-jang	會長	gather + adult/leader = chairman, president
사장 sa-jang	社長	gather + adult/leader = president, CEO
장점 jang-jjeom	長點	long/better + dot/point = advantage, strength
교장 gyo-jang	校長	school + adult/leader = principal, headmaster
장수 jang-su	長壽	long + life = longevity
장남 jang-nam	長男	leader + man/son = the oldest son
가장 ga-jang	家長	house + adult/leader = head of the family, breadwinner
대장 dae-jang	隊長	group + adult/leader = group leader, leader of the pack
성장 seong-jang	成長	achieve + long/adult = growth
장관 jang-gwan	長官	adult/leader + government position = minister

Sample Sentences

저는 이 회사 사장(社長)입니다. = I am the president of this company.

이 친구는 장점(長點)이 많아요. = My friend here has many strong points.

교장(校長) 선생님을 만났어요. = I met the principal.

 사 die

Track 15

Broken bones (歹) and an old man (匕) can only mean 'death.'

Character	Pronunciation	Meaning
死	사 [sa]	die

Breakdown

死	歹	알	broken bone/bad

Footnote
"歹" represents broken bones without any flesh.

死	匕	비	person

Stroke Order

死 死 死 死 死 死

Examples

사망 sa-mang	死亡	die + fail/die = death
사망률 sa-mang-lyul	死亡率	death + ratio = death rate
사망자 sa-mang-ja	死亡者	death + person = the dead, dead person
사형 sa-hyeong	死刑	die + penalty = death penalty
사별 sa-byeol	死別	die + separation = separation by death

Sample Sentences

10명이 사망(死亡)했습니다. = 10 people died.

사망률(死亡率)이 높아졌습니다. = The death rate has become higher.

저 사람은 부모와 사별(死別)했습니다. = That person lost their parents.

Review Quiz

1. Match the character to its sound!

ㄱ. 長   a. 화

ㄴ. 老   b. 노

ㄷ. 北   c. 장

ㄹ. 化   d. 북

2. What does this character mean?

花   =   (   )

3. Find the character that is common among the following words and choose its English meaning.

死亡率 사망률   死刑 사형   死亡 사망   死別 사별

a. long/elder   b. old   c. change   d. die

Answers: 1. ㄱ-c ㄴ-b ㄷ-d ㄹ-a   2. flower   3. d

Flow Chart

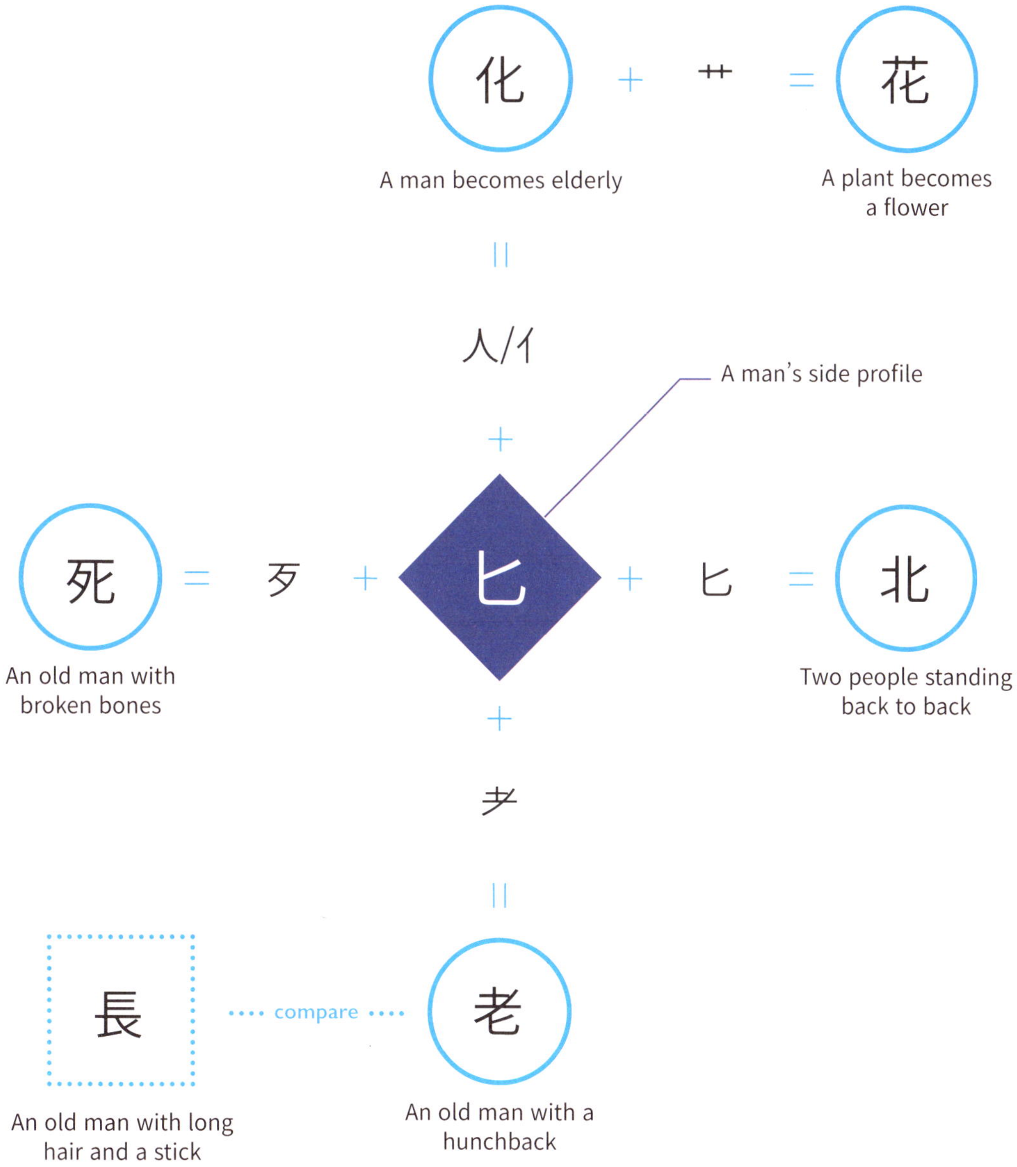

化 + ⺾ = 花

A man becomes elderly   A plant becomes a flower

=

人/亻

+

死 = 歹 + 匕 + 匕 = 北

A man's side profile

An old man with broken bones   Two people standing back to back

+

毛

=

長 ···· compare ···· 老

An old man with long hair and a stick   An old man with a hunchback

Learn Essential Chinese Characters Used in the Korean Language

자 child / suffix

 Track 16

A child wrapped in a blanket means 'sons and daughters', but more often 'son' than 'daughter' as Korean tradition preferred sons. This character is sometimes used as a meaningless suffix, too.

Character	Pronunciation	Meaning
子	자 [ja]	child, suffix, son, person

 Stroke Order

子　子　子

Examples

한글	漢字	의미
자식 ja-sik	子息	child + child = offspring
손자 son-ja	孫子	offspring + son = grandson
여자 yeo-ja	女子	female + person = woman
남자 nam-ja	男子	male + person = man
제자 je-ja	弟子	student + person = student
이자 i-ja	利子	beneficial/interest + suffix = interest
의자 ui-ja	倚子	chair + suffix = chair
액자 aek-jja	額子	frame + suffix = frame
과자 gwa-ja	菓子	snacks + suffix = snacks
왕자 wang-ja	王子	king + son = prince

Sample Sentences

여기는 여자(女子) 화장실이에요. = Here is the women's restroom.

은행 이자(利子)가 높아요. = The bank's interest rate is high.

이 과자(菓子) 정말 맛있어요. = This snack is really tasty.

 study

 Track 17

This character shows that a boy (子) is learning by watching men cover a roof (冖) with bundles (メ) of hay using their hands (臼).

Character	Pronunciation	Meaning
學	학 [hak]	study, learn, school

✂ Breakdown

Character		Pronunciation	Meaning
學	臼	구	both hands
學	メ	symbol	twisted straw rope
學	冖	멱	cover
學	子	자	child

✏ Stroke Order

Examples

학교 hak-kkyo	學校	learn + school = school
학생 hak-ssaeng	學生	learn + be born/person = student
입학 i-pak	入學	enter + learn/school = getting into school
대학교 dae-hak-kkyo	大學校	big + school = university
고등학교 go-deung-hak-kkyo	高等學校	high + level + school = high school
중학교 jung-hak-kkyo	中學校	middle + school = middle school
초등학교 cho-deung-hak-kkyo	初等學校	beginning + level + school = elementary school
방학 bang-hak	放學	let go + learn/school = vacation
학년 hang-nyeon	學年	learn/study + year = grade
유학 yu-hak	留學	stay + learn/study = studying abroad

Sample Sentences

작년에 대학교(大學校)를 졸업했어요. = I graduated from college last year.

저는 중학교(中學校) 2학년이에요. = I am in my second year of middle school.

여름 방학(放學)에 제주도에 가요. = I go to Jeju Island during summer vacation.

 teach

 Track 18

The meaning 'to teach' came from a scene where a child (子) observes the adults linking the roofs together. The adults give the child a lesson in linking the roofs by giving him a straw rope (爻) to twist (攵) together.

Character	Pronunciation	Meaning
敎	교 [gyo]	teach

✂ Breakdown

敎	爻 → 爻	symbol	twisted straw rope
敎	子	자	child
敎	攵	복	strike

Footnote
"攵" means 'strike' because it represents a hand (又) holding a club (丨).

✏ Stroke Order

敎 敎 敎 敎 敎 敎 敎 敎
敎 敎 敎

Examples

교수 gyo-su	教授	teach + give = professor
교사 gyo-sa	教師	teach + teacher = teacher
교실 gyo-sil	教室	teach + house/room = class
교과서 gyo-gwa-seo	教科書	teach + subject + book = textbook
교육 gyo-yuk	教育	teach + raise = education
종교 jong-gyo	宗教	denomination + teach = religion

Sample Sentences

종교(宗教)가 뭐예요? = What is your religion?

교과서(教科書)를 안 가져왔어요. = I didn't bring my textbook.

교실(教室)에 학생이 많아요. = There are many students in the classroom.

 녀 woman

Track 19

A woman sitting with her hands on her knees.

Character	Pronunciation	Meaning
女	녀 [nyeo]	woman, daughter

 Stroke Order

女　女　女

Examples

여자 yeo-ja	女子	woman + person = woman
자녀 ja-nyeo	子女	son + daughter = children
소녀 so-nyeo	少女	small + woman = girl
여왕 yeo-wang	女王	woman + king = queen
마녀 ma-nyeo	魔女	devil + woman = witch
효녀 hyo-nyeo	孝女	filial duty + woman = filial daughter
미녀 mi-nyeo	美女	beautiful + won.an = beautiful woman
처녀 cheo-nyeo	處女	unmarried + woman = single woman
여학생 yeo-hak-ssaeng	女學生	woman + student = female student

Sample Sentences

여기는 여자(女子)만 쓰는 휴게실이에요.
= Here is a girls-only lounge.

자녀(子女)가 몇 명이세요?
= How many children do you have?

이 학교는 남학생보다 여학생(女學生)이 많아요.
= This school has more female students than male students.

호 good

Track 20

It's always a 'good' thing for a mother (女) to hold her child (子).

Character	Pronunciation	Meaning
好	호 [ho]	good, like

✂ **Breakdown**

| 好 | 女 | 녀 | woman |
| 好 | 子 | 자 | child |

✏ **Stroke Order**

好 好 好 好 好 好

Examples

동호회 dong-ho-hoe	同好會	same + like + gather = club, society
선호 seo-no	選好	select + like = preference
호감 ho-gam	好感	like + feel = having a good feeling, likeable
양호 yang-ho	良好	benevolent + good = satisfactory, fine

Sample Sentences

사진 동호회(同好會)에 들었어요. = I joined a photography club.

선호(選好)하는 색깔이 있어요? = Do you have a color that you prefer?

저 사람한테 호감(好感)이 있어요. = I feel attracted to that person.

 요 necessary / essential

A woman (女) is standing while supporting her waist with two hands (襾→臼). Derived to mean essential or need as the waist is the most critical part of the body.

Character	Pronunciation	Meaning
要	요 [yo]	necessary, essential, demand, desire

✂ Breakdown

要	襾→臼	symbol	two hands

Footnote
An ancient version of this character shows "襾" as a shape of "two hands 臼."

要	女	녀	woman

✏ Stroke Order

要 要 要 要 要 要 要 要 要

Examples

필요 pi-ryo	必要	certainly + essential = need
요청 yo-cheong	要請	essential + ask = request
중요 jung-yo	重要	heavy + essential = important
강요 gang-yo	強要	strong + demand = pressure, coercion
요령 yo-ryeong	要領	essential + point = trick, know-how
수요 su-yo	需要	things needed + desire = demand
요약 yo-yak	要約	essential + bundle up = sum up

Sample Sentences

오늘 중요(重要)한 시험이 있어요. = I have an important exam today.

자꾸 하면 요령(要領)이 생겨요. = If you keep doing it, you will develop some know-how.

내용을 간단히 요약(要約)했어요. = I summed up the content briefly.

 모 mother

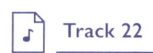 Track 22

Turn the character for woman (女) on its side, add two dots (丶, 丶) to indicate breastfeeding, and the character means 'mother.'

Character	Pronunciation	Meaning
母	모 [mo]	mother, woman around mother's age

✏️ Stroke Order

Examples

학부모 hak-ppu-mo	學父母	learn/school + father + mother = student's parent
모교 mo-gyo	母校	mother + school = alma mater
모음 mo-eum	母音	mother + sound = vowel
모자 mo-ja	母子	mother + son = mother and son
모녀 mo-nyeo	母女	mother + daughter = mother and daughter
고모 go-mo	姑母	father's sister + woman around mother's age = father's sister, aunt
이모 i-mo	姨母	mother's sister + woman around mother's age = mother's sister, aunt
모국어 mo-gu-geo	母國語	mother + country + word = mother tongue
유모차 yu-mo-cha	乳母車	milk + mother + wagon/cart = stroller

Sample Sentences

여기가 제 모교(母校)예요.　　　　= This is my alma mater.

영어가 제 모국어(母國語)예요.　　= English is my mother tongue.

아기는 유모차(乳母車) 안에 있어요.　= The baby is in the stroller.

Review Quiz

1. Match the character to its sound!

ㄱ. 母		a. 자	
ㄴ. 好		b. 모	
ㄷ. 要		c. 교	
ㄹ. 子		d. 호	
ㅁ. 敎		e. 요	

2. What does this character mean?

女　　＝　　(　　　　　　)

3. Find the character that is common among the following words and choose its English meaning.

> 學校학교　　學生학생　　放學방학　　學年학년

a. mother　　b. teach　　c. necessary/essential　　d. study

Answers: 1. ㄱ-b ㄴ-d ㄷ-e ㄹ-a ㅁ-c　　2. woman　　3. d

Flow Chart

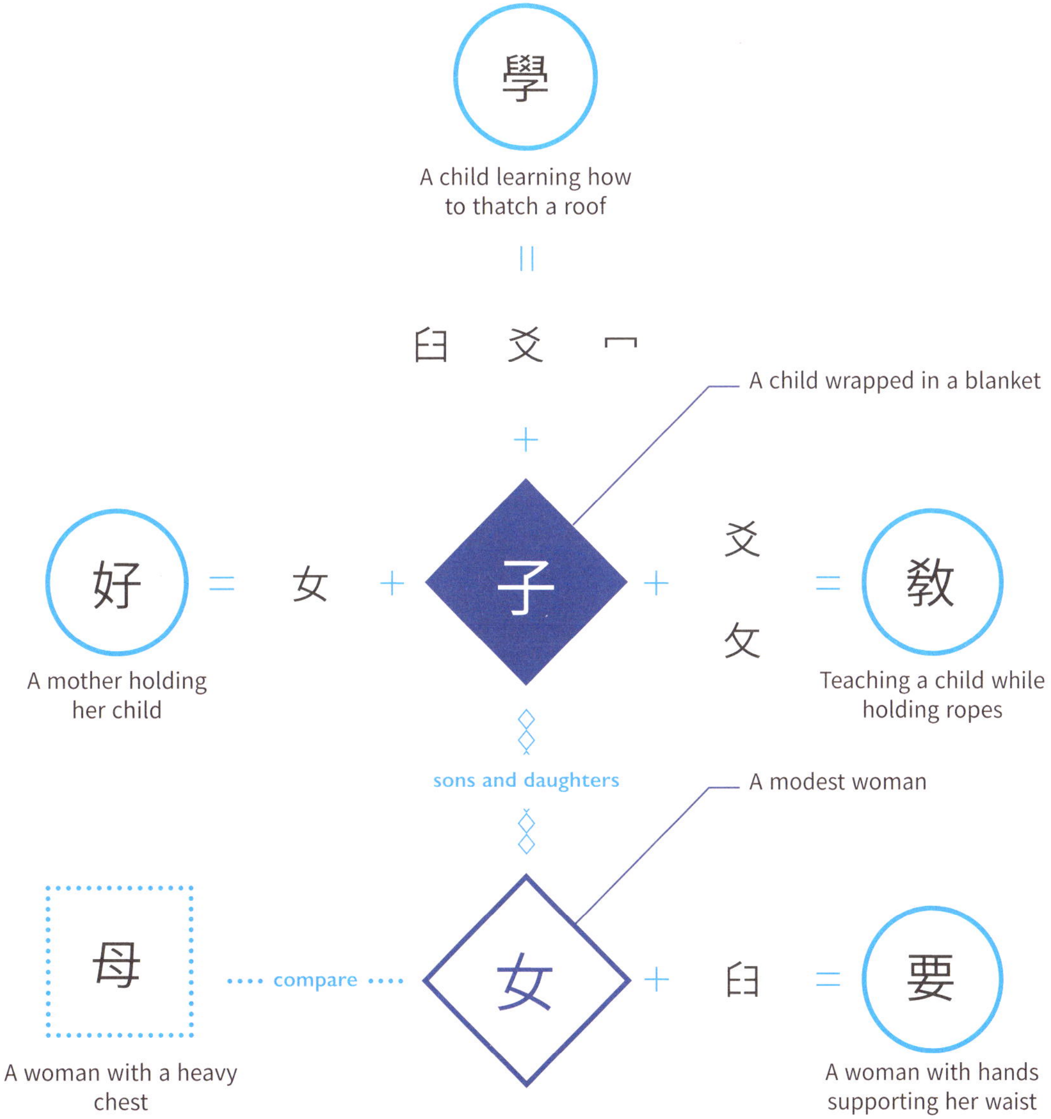

學
A child learning how to thatch a roof

=

臼 爻 冖

+

子 — A child wrapped in a blanket

好 = 女 + 子 + 爻/攵 = 教

A mother holding her child

Teaching a child while holding ropes

sons and daughters

A modest woman

母 ···· compare ···· 女 + 臼 = 要

A woman with a heavy chest

A woman with hands supporting her waist

Learn Essential Chinese Characters Used in the Korean Language

Body

身 — 大 — 美 — 文 — 自 — 辛 — 親 — 新 —

意 — 口 — 名 — 品 — 加 — 國 — 民 — 古 —

高 — 中 — 結 — 心 — 必 — 性 — 愛 — 情 —

 신 body

 Track 23

A side profile of a pregnant woman's body.

Character	Pronunciation	Meaning
身	신 [sin]	body

Stroke Order

Examples

자신 ja-sin	自身	oneself + body = oneself
대신 dae-sin	代身	substitute + body = instead
출신 chul-ssin	出身	be born/go out + body = origin
신분 sin-bun	身分	body + position/status = position, status
변신 byeon-sin	變身	change + body = transformation
망신 mang-sin	亡身	fail + body = shame
전신 jeon-sin	全身	whole + body = whole body
독신 dok-ssin	獨身	alone + body = unmarried person, single

Sample Sentences

커피 대신(代身) 차를 마셨어요.   = I drank tea instead of coffee.

그 사람은 서울 출신(出身)이에요.   = He is from Seoul.

저는 독신(獨身)이에요.   = I am single.

 대 big

 Track 24

A person (人) with their limbs spread out (一). This character is just another form of 'person.'

Character	Pronunciation	Meaning
大	대 [dae]	big, large

 Stroke Order

Examples

대학 dae-hak	大學	big + school = university
확대 hwak-ttae	擴大	expand + big = expansion, enlargement
대통령 dae-tong-lyeong	大統領	big + command + govern = president
최대 choe-dae	最大	most + big = most, biggest
대기업 dae-gi-eop	大企業	big + company = major company
대회 dae-hoe	大會	big + gather = large meeting, competition
대중 dae-jung	大衆	big + group = public

Sample Sentences

이 부분 확대(擴大)해 볼래요? = Can you try expanding this part?

대기업(大企業)에서 일해요. = I work in a big company.

내일 체육 대회(大會)가 있어요. = Tomorrow we have an athletics competition.

 미 beautiful

 Track 25

A man (大) carrying a sheep (羊) as an offering to the gods was considered a 'beautiful or grand' sight.

Character	Pronunciation	Meaning
美	미 [mi]	beautiful

Breakdown

美	羊	양	sheep
美	大	대	person/big

Stroke Order

美 美 美 美 美 美 美 美
美

Examples

미술 mi-sul	美術	beautiful + skill = art, fine art
미인 mi-in	美人	beautiful + person = beautiful woman
미남 mi-nam	美男	beautiful + man = handsome man
미용실 mi-yong-sil	美容室	beautiful + face + house/room = beauty salon
미식가 mi-sik-kka	美食家	beautiful + meal/eat + person = gourmet

Sample Sentences

저는 미술(美術)을 전공했어요. = I majored in fine art.

제 친구 미인(美人)이죠? = My friend is pretty, right?

어제 미용실(美容室)에서 파마를 했어요. = I got a perm at a beauty salon yesterday.

 character / script

Track 26

A man with a tattoo on his chest (乂), which is below the head (亠). Chinese characters began as drawings similar to tattoos, so this character came to mean 'character or writing.'

Character	Pronunciation	Meaning
文	문 [mun]	character, script, writing, sentence

✎ Stroke Order

Examples

문화 mu-nwa	文化	writing + change = culture
주문 ju-mun	注文	annotate/write down + sentence = order
문자 mun-jja	文字	character + letter/character = letter
문장 mun-jang	文章	sentence + sentence = sentence
문학 mu-nak	文學	writing + learn/study = literature
문법 mun-ppeop	文法	writing + law = grammar
문맹 mun-maeng	文盲	character + blind = illiteracy
예문 ye-mun	例文	example + sentence = sample sentence

Sample Sentences

인터넷으로 책을 주문(注文)했어요. = I ordered a book online.

이 문장(文章)을 100번 쓰세요. = Write this sentence 100 times.

다음 예문(例文)을 읽어 보세요. = Read the following sample sentence.

자 oneself

 Track 27

The nose is the most prominent feature of a face. The character for 'oneself' is borrowed from the image of a nose. When someone points to indicate himself or herself, they usually point at their own nose.

Character	Pronunciation	Meaning
自	자 [ja]	oneself

Sidenote

A nose appears in a lot of sayings or proverbs about pride or arrogance. This further indicates that a nose can mean oneself.

 Stroke Order

Examples

자동차 ja-dong-cha	自動車	oneself + move + vehicle = car
자전거 ja-jeon-geo	自轉車	oneself + roll + vehicle = bicycle
자유 ja-yu	自由	oneself + come from = freedom
자연 ja-yeon	自然	oneself + so/such = nature
자존심 ja-jon-sim	自尊心	oneself + high + mind = self-esteem
각자 gak-jja	各自	each + oneself = each, respectively
자신감 ja-sin-gam	自信感	oneself + believe/trust + feel = self-confidence
자살 ja-sal	自殺	oneself + to kill = suicide

Sample Sentences

자동차(自動車)로 20분 걸려요. = It takes 20 minutes by car.

저는 자전거(自轉車)를 못 타요. = I can't ride a bicycle.

자신감(自信感)을 가져요. = Have some confidence.

Review Quiz

1. Match the character to its sound!

ㄱ. 自 　　　　　　a. 자

ㄴ. 文 　　　　　　b. 미

ㄷ. 身 　　　　　　c. 문

ㄹ. 美 　　　　　　d. 신

2. What does this character mean?

美　=　(　　　　　)

3. Find the character that is common among the following words and choose its English meaning.

大會대회　　大統領대통령　　大學대학　　大企業대기업

a. oneself　　b. big　　c. body　　d. character/script

Answers:　1. ㄱ-a ㄴ-c ㄷ-d ㄹ-b　　2. beautiful　　3. b

80　　Your First Hanja Guide

Flow Chart

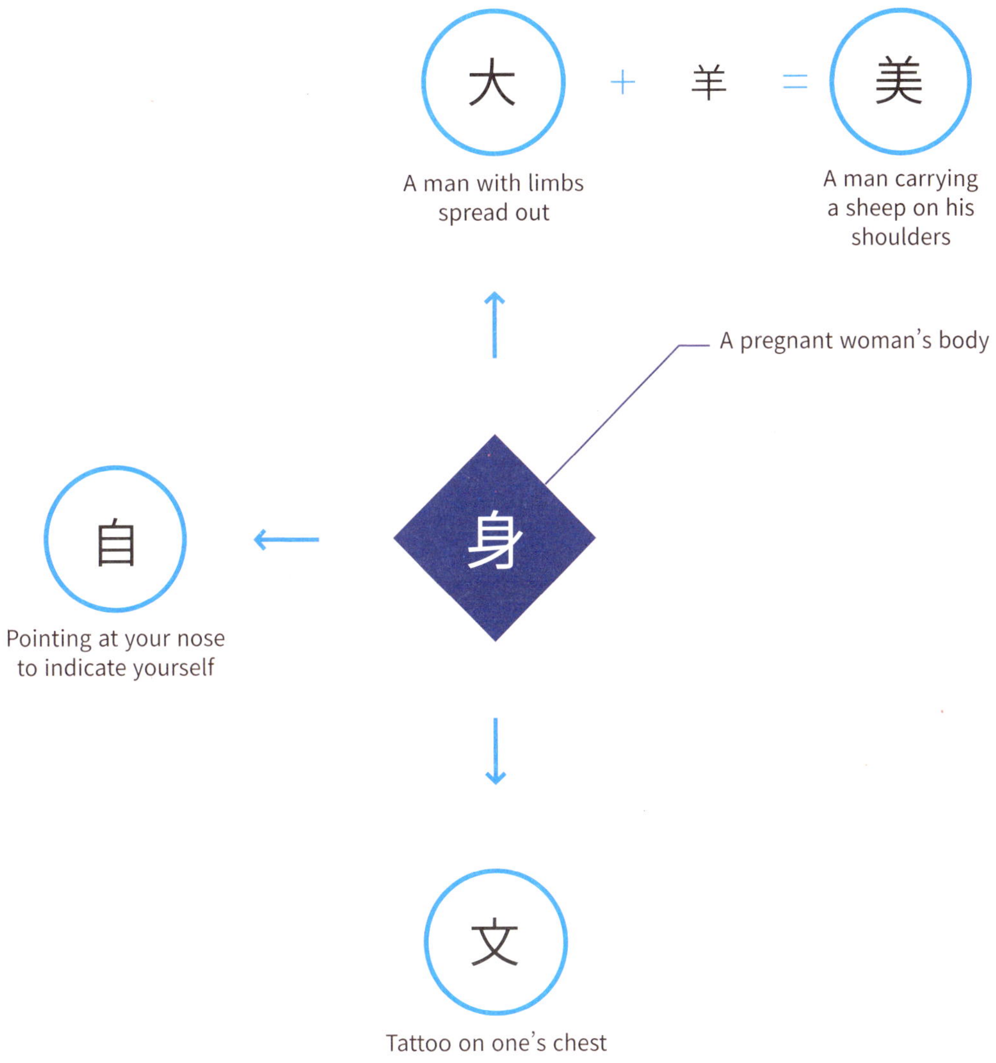

大 + 羊 = 美

A man with limbs spread out

A man carrying a sheep on his shoulders

A pregnant woman's body

身

自

Pointing at your nose to indicate yourself

文

Tattoo on one's chest

 신 **pain / pungent**

 Track 28

The shape of an awl, a long and sharp tool, signifies pain. It also means 'spicy', a taste that can be described as painful. This character is not related to "stand 立 [립]."

Character	Pronunciation	Meaning
辛	신 [sin]	pain, pungent, spicy

Sidenote

"立" - A man (person/big 大) standing with two feet firmly on the ground (一).

Stroke Order

Examples

향신료
hyang-sin-nyo

香辛料   scent + spicy + count/material = spice

Sample Sentences

이 요리에 어떤 향신료(香辛料)가 들어가요?   = What kind of spice goes into this dish?

 친 intimate / parent

 Track 29

This character shows a parent watching (見) their child and disciplining them with an awl (辛) so the child will grow up (木) well.

Character	Pronunciation	Meaning
親	친 [chin]	intimate, parent, friendly, in person

✂ Breakdown

親	立→辛	신	awl/pain
親	木	목	tree
親	見	견	see

✏ Stroke Order

親 親 親 親 親 親 親 親
親 親 親 親 親 親 親 親

Examples

친구 chin-gu	親舊	intimate + long time = friend
친척 chin-cheok	親戚	parent + relative = relative
친절 chin-jeol	親切	friendly + sincere = kind
친필 chin-pil	親筆	in person + brush/write = handwriting
친환경 chi-nwan-gyeong	親環境	friendly + environment = environmentally-friendly

Sample Sentences

친한 친구(親舊)가 몇 명이에요? = How many close friends do you have?

친척(親戚) 집에 놀러 왔어요. = I came to visit my relative.

친환경(親環境) 세제를 써요. = I use environmentally-friendly detergent.

 신 new

 Track 30

If disciplining with an awl (辛) fails to help something become worthy (木), then one must take an ax (斤) to cut off the decaying branches and help new ones grow.

Character	Pronunciation	Meaning
新	신 [sin]	new

Breakdown

新	立→辛	신	awl/pain
新	木	목	tree
新	斤	근	ax

Stroke Order

新 新 新 新 新 新 新 新
新 新 新 新 新

Examples

한글	漢字	뜻
신문 sin-mun	新聞	new + hear = newspaper
신제품 sin-je-pum	新製品	new + make + thing/stuff = new product
신입 si-nip	新入	new + enter = newcomer, new member
신입생 si-nip-ssaeng	新入生	new + enter + person = new student, freshman, first year student
신랑 sil-lang	新郎	new + man/husband = groom
신부 sin-bu	新婦	new + wife = bride
최신 choi-sin	最新	most + new = the newest, the latest
신인 si-nin	新人	new + person = rookie
신학기 si-nak-kki	新學期	new + learn/school + term = new semester
신생아 sin-saeng-a	新生兒	new + be born + child/baby = newborn baby

Sample Sentences

오늘 신문(新聞) 봤어요?   = Have you seen today's newspaper?

신인(新人) 가수 진석진입니다.   = I'm rookie singer Seokjin Jin.

신입(新入) 사원 언제 뽑아요?   = When are you hiring new employees?

 meaning

Track 31

What the heart (心) says (音) is what one truly means.

Character	Pronunciation	Meaning
意	의 [ui]	meaning, mind

Breakdown

意	音	음	sound

Footnote
Ancient Chinese texts show that "word 言" and "sound 音" have something to do with blowing into an instrument. At first they were used interchangeably until "音" came to stress sound and "言" was used to stress context.

意	心	심	heart

Stroke Order

意 意 意 意 意 意 意 意
意 意 意 意 意

Examples

의미 ui-mi	意味	meaning + meaning = meaning
의견 ui-gyeon	意見	mind + view = opinion
의지 ui-ji	意志	meaning/mind + meaning/mind = will
합의 ha-bui	合意	combine + mind = agreement
주의 ju-ui	注意	pour + mind = caution, attention
고의 go-ui	故意	deliberately + mind = on purpose, intention
성의 seong-ui	誠意	sincere + mind = sincerity, sincere effort

Sample Sentences

두 명의 의견(意見)이 아주 달라요. = The two people's opinions are very different.

의지(意志)가 강한 사람이에요. = He is a man who has a strong will.

이 점 꼭 주의(注意)하세요. = Make sure you keep this in mind.

Review Quiz

1. Match the character to its sound!

ㄱ. 意　　　　　　　　a. 신

ㄴ. 親　　　　　　　　b. 의

ㄷ. 辛　　　　　　　　c. 친

2. What does this character mean?

辛　＝　(　　　　　　)

3. Find the character that is common among the following words and choose its English meaning.

新入生 신입생　　　新製品 신제품
新生兒 신생아　　　新聞 신문

a. meaning　　b. parent　　c. new　　d. intimate

Answers:　1. ㄱ-b ㄴ-c ㄷ-a　2. pain / pungent　3. c

Flow Chart

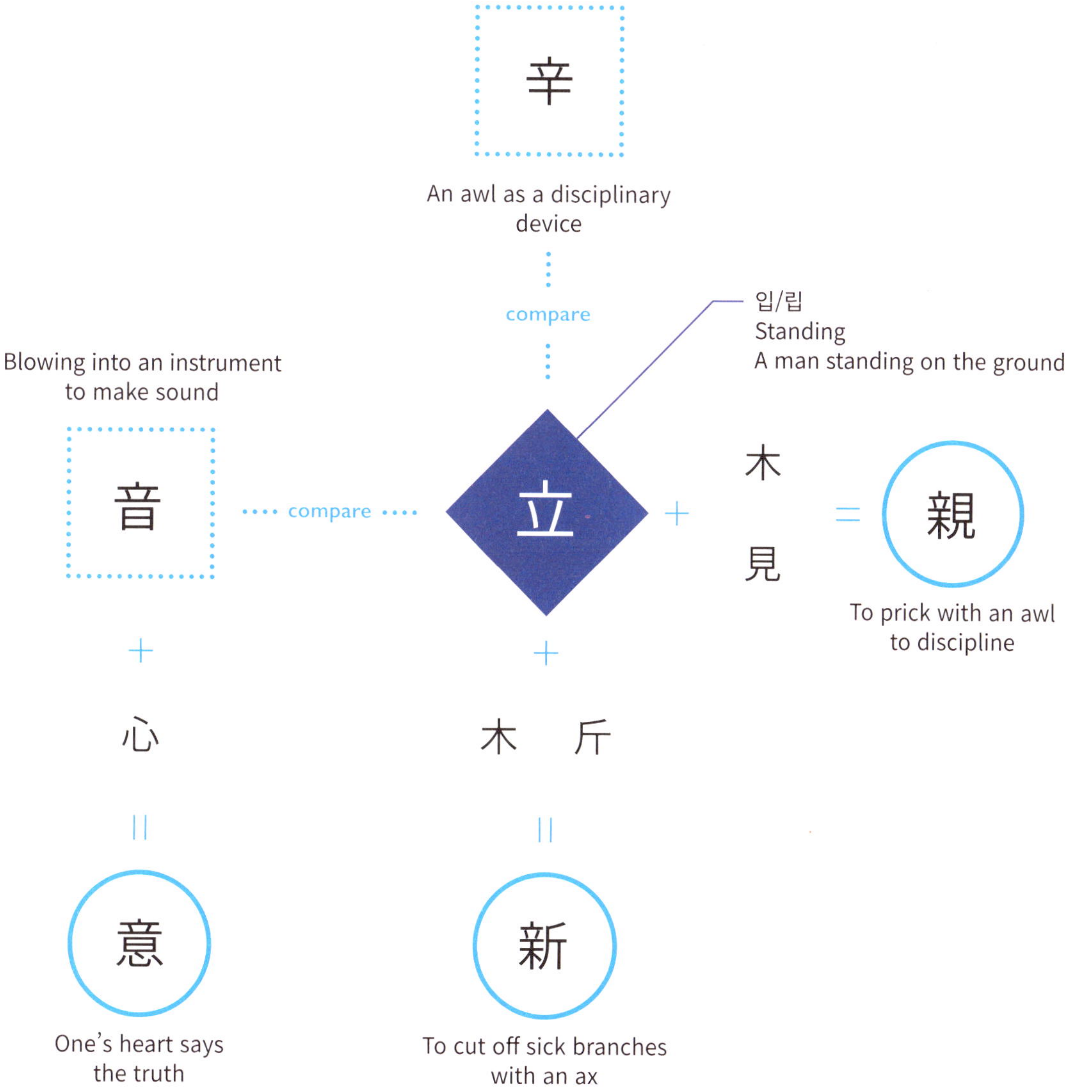

辛
An awl as a disciplinary device

⋯⋯ compare ⋯⋯

Blowing into an instrument to make sound

音 ⋯⋯ compare ⋯⋯ 立 + 木 見 = 親

입/립
Standing
A man standing on the ground

To prick with an awl to discipline

+ 心 = 意
One's heart says the truth

+ 木 斤 = 新
To cut off sick branches with an ax

Learn Essential Chinese Characters Used in the Korean Language

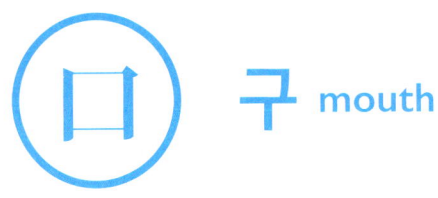 mouth

 Track 32

The shape of a mouth. When used as part of another character, it describes an action done with a mouth, like 'eat, speak, or cry.' Be careful however, as there are characters that look like "口" but have a different meaning.

Character	Pronunciation	Meaning
口	구 [gu]	mouth

Sidenote

Chinese characters have changed over the centuries. Therefore, there exist numerous characters which look similar but originate from different sources. Just because the two characters look the same, it doesn't necessarily mean that they have the same meaning.

Stroke Order

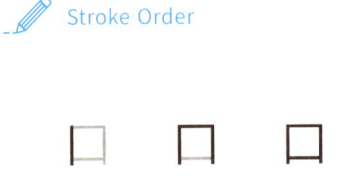

Examples

입구 ip-kku	入口	enter + mouth = entrance
출구 chul-gu	出口	go out + mouth = exit
식구 sik-kku	食口	eat + mouth = family member
인구 in-gu	人口	person + mouth = population
비상구 bi-sang-gu	非常口	not + always + mouth/door = emergency exit
창구 chang-gu	窓口	window + mouth = counter
항구 hang-gu	港口	harbor + mouth = harbor

Sample Sentences

출구(出口)를 못 찾겠어요. = I can't find the exit.

저희 집은 식구(食口)가 많아요. = We have a lot of people in our family.

비상구(非常口)는 이쪽 끝에 있어요. = The emergency exit is at the end this way.

 name

 Track 33

In the middle of a dark night (夕), one must call (口) out names of others to find or recognize them.

Character	Pronunciation	Meaning
名	명 [myeong]	name

✂ Breakdown

名	夕	석	evening

Footnote
"夕" represents the shape of a crescent moon, signifying evening.

名	口	구	mouth

✏ Stroke Order

名　名　名　名　名　名

Examples

유명 yu-myeong	有名	exist/have + name = famous
명절 myeong-jeol	名節	name + anniversary/holiday = (national) holiday
서명 seo-myeong	署名	government office + name = signature
명문 myeong-mun	名門	name + door = prestigious
명예 myeong-ye	名譽	name + praise = honor
지명 ji-myeong	地名	place + name = place name
익명 ing-myeong	匿名	hide + name = anonymous
누명 nu-myeong	陋名	dirty + name = false charge
가명 ga-myeong	假名	lie + name = alias, pseudonym
실명 sil-myeong	實名	truly + name = autonym, real name
명품 myeong-pum	名品	name + product = masterpiece, brand-name product

Sample Sentences

제주도는 관광지로 유명(有名)해요. = Jeju Island is famous as a tourist site.

익명(匿名)의 편지가 왔어요. = I received an anonymous letter.

제 친구가 누명(陋名)을 썼어요. = My friend was framed.

품 article / object

Track 34

An image of people commenting (口) on a single product.

Character	Pronunciation	Meaning
品	품 [pum]	article, object, product, stuff, quality

Breakdown

品	口	구	mouth
品	口	구	mouth
品	口	구	mouth

Stroke Order

Examples

작품 jak-pum	作品	make + stuff = work (of art)
화장품 hwa-jang-pum	化粧品	makeup + product = cosmetics
제품 je-pum	製品	make + stuff = product
식품 sik-pum	食品	eat + stuff = food
품질 pum-jil	品質	product + quality = quality
성품 seong-pum	性品	personality + quality = personality, character
경품 gyeong-pum	景品	happy + product = prize, giveaway prize
기념품 gi-nyeom-pum	紀念品	era + think/remember + product = souvenir

Sample Sentences

생일 선물로 화장품(化粧品)을 받았어요. = I got cosmetics for my birthday.

수건을 경품(景品)으로 받았어요. = I received a towel as a prize.

기념품(紀念品) 샀어요? = Did you buy souvenirs?

 가 add

 Track 35

Farmers plowing (力) their fields, using their mouths (口) to shout or sing, add more power (力) to each stroke or push they give.

Character	Pronunciation	Meaning
加	가 [ga]	add

✂ Breakdown

加	力	력	plow/power

Footnote
"力" - Symbolizes plow, a critical tool in agriculture. Power is needed to pull the plow in the fields.

加	口	구	mouth

✏ Stroke Order

加 加 加 加 加

Examples

| 추가
chu-ga | 追加 | pursue/fill + add = addition |

| 참가
cham-ga | 參加 | participate + add = participation |

| 증가
jeung-ga | 增加 | add/increase + add = increase |

| 가입
ga-ip | 加入 | add + enter = join |

| 가속
ga-sok | 加速 | add + fast = acceleration |

Sample Sentences

1인분 더 추가(追加)할게요. = I will add one more serving.

마라톤 대회에 참가(參加)하고 싶어요. = I want to participate in the marathon competition.

테니스 모임에 가입(加入)했어요. = I joined a tennis group.

국 country / nation

Track 36

The meaning of 'country, nation' is derived from an image of the people of the country (口) protecting their land (一) by surrounding (口) the boundary of the land with spears (戈).

Character	Pronunciation	Meaning
國	국 [guk]	country, nation

Breakdown

國	口	위	enclose
國	戈	과	spear
國	口	구	mouth
國	一	symbol	land

Stroke Order

國 國 國 國 國 國 國 國
國 國 國

Your First Hanja Guide

Examples

한글	漢字	뜻
국가 guk-kka	國家	country + house = country
국회 gu-koe	國會	country + gather = National Assembly
외국 oe-guk	外國	outside + country = foreign country
외국인 oe-gu-gin	外國人	outside + country + person = foreigner
외국어 oe-gu-geo	外國語	outside + country + word = foreign language
천국 cheon-guk	天國	sky + country = heaven
국사 guk-ssa	國史	country + history = national history
국제 guk-jje	國際	country + relation = international
국내 gung-nae	國內	country + inside = domestic
전국 jeon-guk	全國	whole + country = the whole country

Sample Sentences

외국(外國) 여행은 이번이 처음이에요. = This is my first time traveling to a foreign country.

이태원에는 외국인(外國人)이 정말 많아요. = There are really a lot of foreigners in Itaewon.

오늘 전국(全國)에 비가 내릴 거예요. = It will rain throughout the whole country today.

민 the people / subjects

Track 37

War prisoners were made slaves by blinding them in one eye (目) with a spear (矛). The meaning later changed to 'people.'

Character	Pronunciation	Meaning
民	민 [min]	the people, subjects

✏️ Stroke Order

Examples

한글	漢字	뜻
국민 gung-min	國民	country + the people = nation, people, the public
민간인 min-ga-nin	民間人	the people + gap + person = civilian
민속 min-sok	民俗	the people + custom = folklore
민원 mi-nwon	民願	the people + want/wish = civil complaint
난민 nan-min	難民	difficult/adversity + the people = refugee
민박 min-bak	民泊	the people + stay = bed and breakfast (accommodation)
이민 i-min	移民	move + the people = emigration

Sample Sentences

구청에 민원(民願)을 냈어요. = I filed a civil complaint at the district office.

바다 근처에서 민박(民泊)을 했어요. = I stayed at a bed and breakfast near the sea.

저희 이모는 캐나다로 이민(移民)을 갔어요. = My aunt emigrated to Canada.

Review Quiz

1. Match the character to its sound!

ㄱ. 民		a. 가
ㄴ. 國		b. 국
ㄷ. 加		c. 구
ㄹ. 品		d. 민
ㅁ. 口		e. 품

2. What does this character mean?

口　=　(　　　　　　)

3. Find the character that is common among the following words and choose its English meaning.

實名실명　　假名가명　　匿名익명　　有名유명

a. add　　b. article/object　　c. the people/subjects　　d. name

Answers:　1. ㄱ-d ㄴ-b ㄷ-a ㄹ-e ㅁ-c　2. mouth　3. d

104　　Your First Hanja Guide

Flow Chart

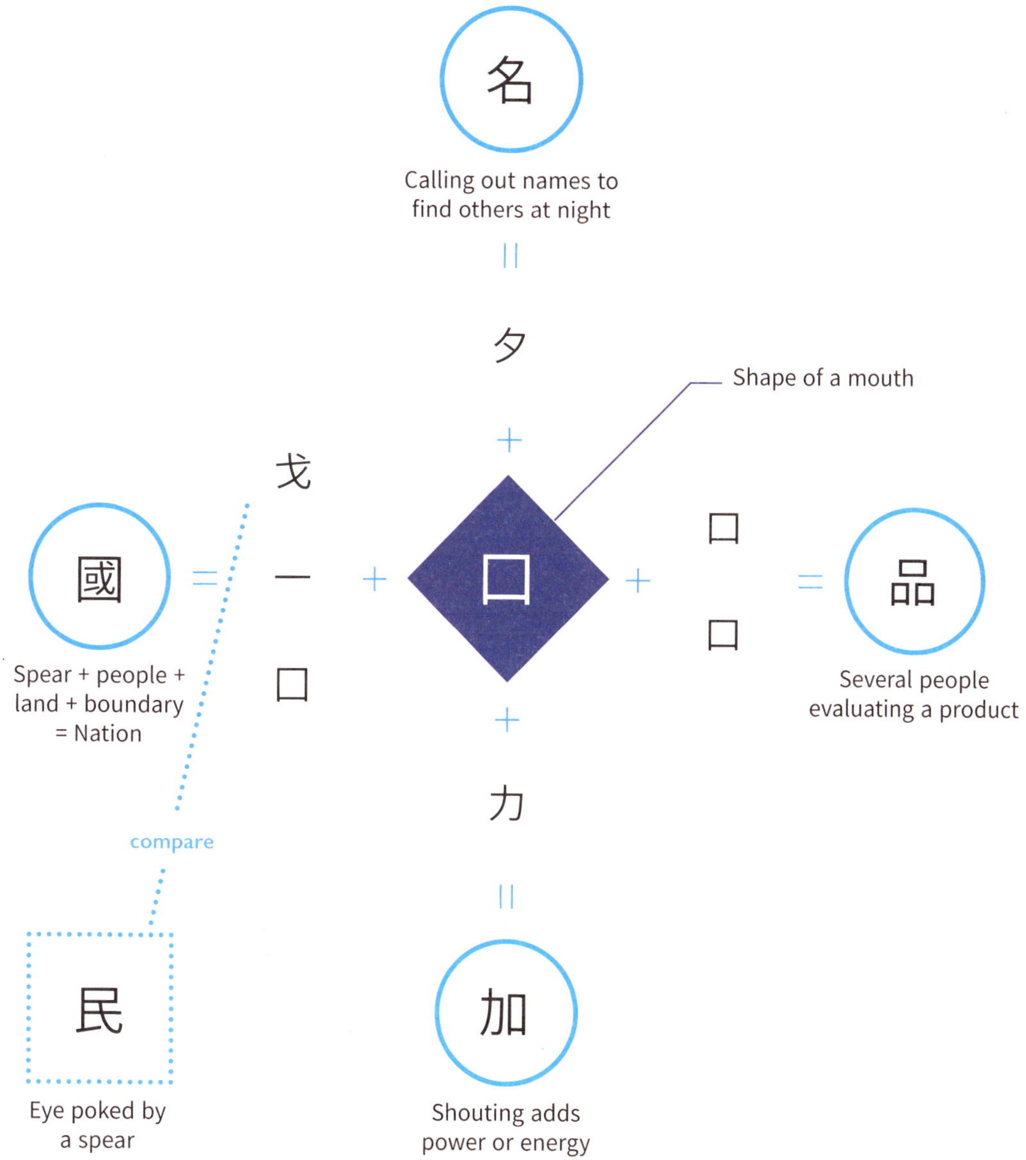

名
Calling out names to find others at night
=
夕
+
口 — Shape of a mouth

國
Spear + people + land + boundary = Nation

= 戈 + 一 + 口

+ 口
口 口
= 品
Several people evaluating a product

compare

民
Eye poked by a spear

+
力
=
加
Shouting adds power or energy

Learn Essential Chinese Characters Used in the Korean Language

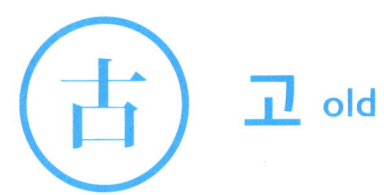 고 old

 Track 38

To put food in a jar (口) and cover with a heavy stone (十), to marinate or ripen the food for a long time.

Character	Pronunciation	Meaning
古	고 [go]	old, the old days

Sidenote

For this character, "口" has a different meaning than 'mouth.' Here, it's the shape of a container.

 Stroke Order

Examples

고물 go-mul	古物	old + object = junk
고참 go-cham	古參	old + participate = senior
복고 bok-kko	復古	get back + the old days = retro
부고 bu-go	赴古	inform/notify + old = a notice of death
고대 go-dae	古代	old + time = ancient
고전 go-jeon	古典	old + book = classic

Sample Sentences

그 고물(古物) 자동차 좀 바꿔요. = Why not change that junk car (to a new one)?

제 고참(古參)은 나이가 저보다 어려요. = My senior is younger than me.

요즘 복고(復古)가 유행이에요. = Retro style is in fashion these days.

 고 high

 Track 39

The shape of a large palace with a wide entrance (⬜) for people to enter and exit through. It means 'high.'

Character	Pronunciation	Meaning
高	고 [go]	high

 Stroke Order

Examples

최고 choe-go	最高	most + high =	the best
고가 go-kka	高價	high + price =	high price
고령 go-ryeong	高齡	high + age =	old age
고속 도로 go-sok do-ro	高速 道路	high + speed + road =	expressway
고액 go-aek	高額	high + amount/figure =	large amount of money
고혈압 go-hyeo-rap	高血壓	high + blood + pressure =	hypertension, high blood pressure

Sample Sentences

우리 아빠가 최고(最高)야. = My dad is the best.

면세점에서 고가(高價)의 가방을 샀어요. = I bought an expensive bag in a duty free shop.

고속 도로(高速 道路)에서 사고가 났어요. = There was an accident on the expressway.

 center

 Track 40

This character describes an object (口) which is pierced (|) in the middle or center.

Character	Pronunciation	Meaning
中	중 [jung]	center, middle

✂ Breakdown

中	口		symbol object
中	|	곤	piercing/penetrating

✏ Stroke Order

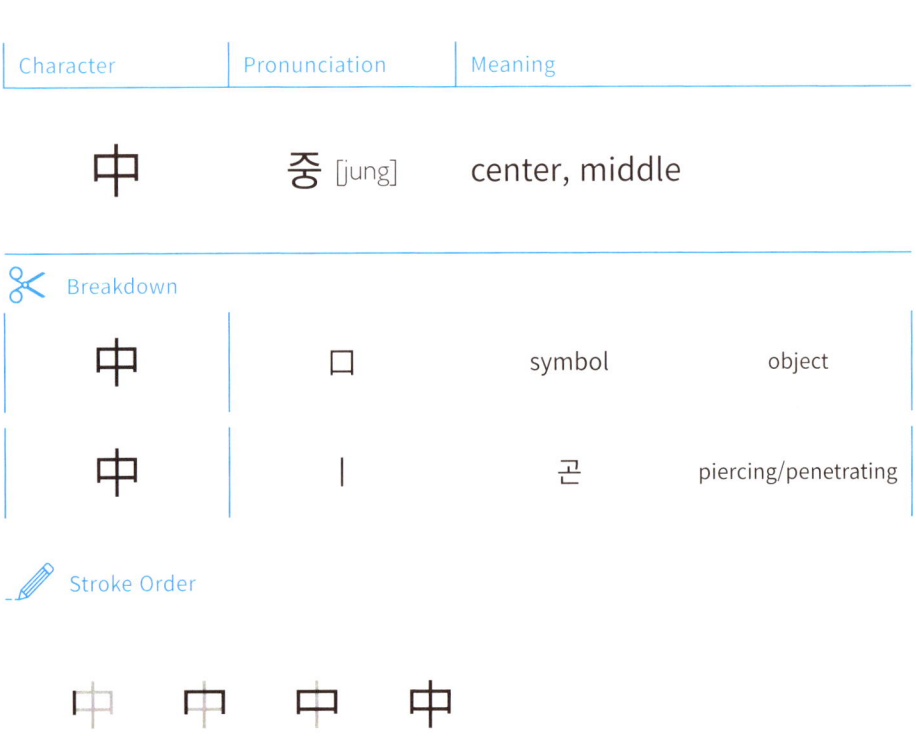

Examples

중심 jung-sim	中心	middle + center = center
중단 jung-dan	中斷	middle + cut = halt, stop
집중 jip-jjung	集中	gather + middle = concentration
중간 jung-gan	中間	middle + gap = middle
중독 jung-dok	中毒	middle + poison = addiction

Sample Sentences

공부에 집중(集中)이 안돼요. = I can't focus on my studies.

여기가 학교와 집의 중간(中間)이에요. = This is the midpoint between school and home.

그 사람은 커피 중독(中毒)이에요. = He is addicted to coffee.

 결 bear (fruit) / tie

 Track 41

To sign or agree to (糸) a peace (吉) treaty means to 'tie' two or more villages together. "糸" is used to tie or connect the parties.

Character	Pronunciation	Meaning
結	결 [gyeol]	bear (fruit), tie

✂ Breakdown

結	糸	사	thread
結	吉	길	peace/lucky

Footnote

"吉" - An ax (士), a symbol of authority and also used as a weapon, is lying neglected on a stand (口). For the handle of an ax to rot away means that there has been peace for many years, which is considered 'lucky'.

✏ Stroke Order

Examples

한글	漢字	분석
결혼 gyeo-ron	結婚	bear/tie + marry = marriage
결혼식 gyeo-ron-sik	結婚式	bear/tie + marry + ceremony = wedding ceremony
결과 gyeol-gwa	結果	bear/tie + fruit/result = result
결론 gyeol-lon	結論	bear/tie + discuss = conclusion
연결 yeon-gyeol	連結	continue + bear/tie = connection
결말 gyeol-mal	結末	bear/tie + end = ending

Sample Sentences

작년에 결혼(結婚)했어요.
= I got married last year.

결혼식(結婚式)은 언제 해요?
= When are you having your wedding ceremony?

결과(結果)보다는 과정이 중요해요.
= The process is more important than the result.

Review Quiz

1. Match the character to its sound!

ㄱ. 古　　　　　　　　　a. 고

ㄴ. 中　　　　　　　　　b. 결

ㄷ. 結　　　　　　　　　c. 중

2. What does this character mean?

中　＝　(　　　　　　　)

3. Find the character that is common among the following words and choose its English meaning.

最高최고　　高價고가
高血壓고혈압　　高額고액

a. tie　　b. high　　c. old　　d. bear (fruit)

Answers: 1. ㄱ-a ㄴ-c ㄷ-b　2. center　3. b

Flow Chart

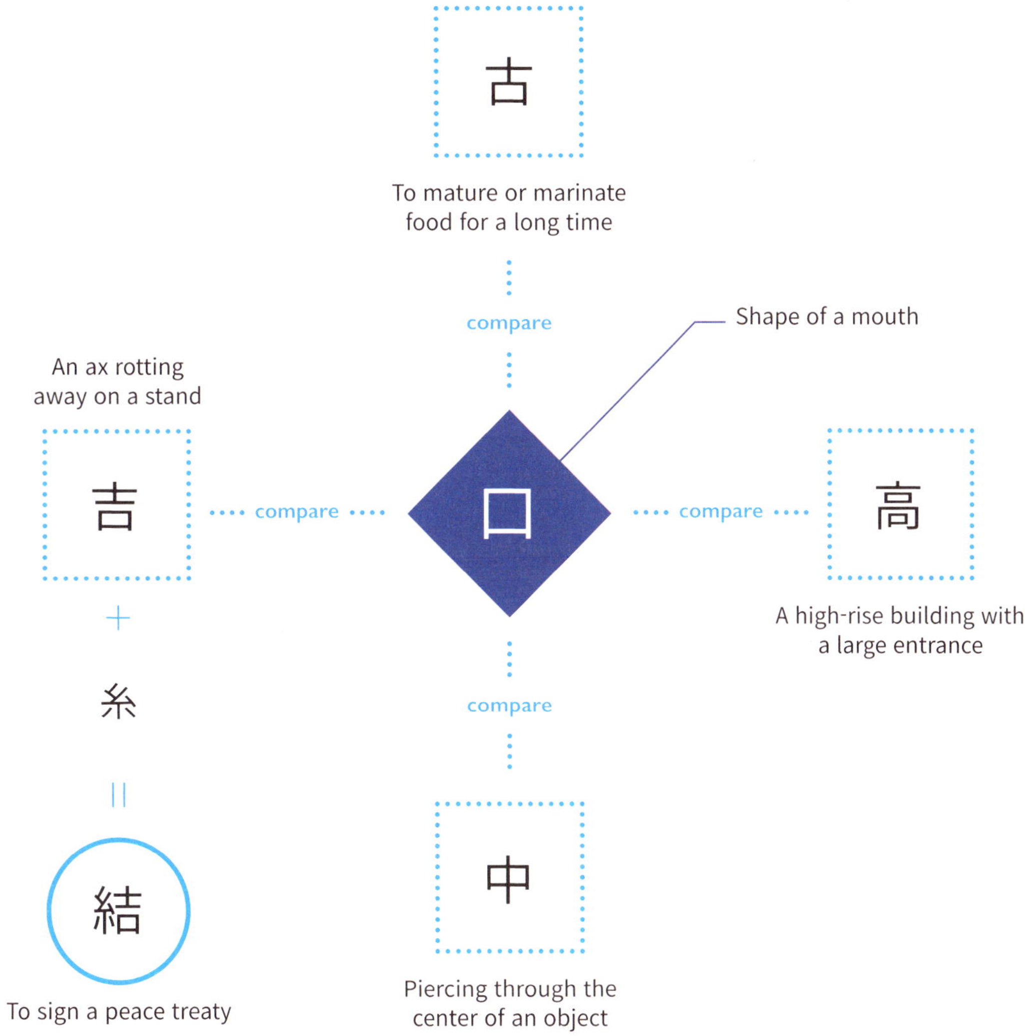

古

To mature or marinate food for a long time

compare

Shape of a mouth

An ax rotting away on a stand

吉 ···· compare ···· 口 ···· compare ···· 高

A high-rise building with a large entrance

+

糸

=

結

To sign a peace treaty

compare

中

Piercing through the center of an object

Learn Essential Chinese Characters Used in the Korean Language

 심 mind / heart

 Track 42

This character is a pictograph of a heart, but in other characters it symbolizes emotions or characteristics.

Character	Pronunciation	Meaning
心/忄	심 [sim]	mind, heart

Stroke Order

Examples

심장 sim-jang	心臟	mind/heart + organ = heart
중심 jung-sim	中心	middle + mind/heart = center
의심 ui-sim	疑心	doubt/suspect + mind = doubt

관심 gwan-sim	關心	relate with + mind = interest
핵심 haek-ssim	核心	seed + heart = core
조심 jo-sim	操心	hold + mind = being careful
자존심 ja-jon-sim	自尊心	oneself + respect + mind = self-esteem
한심 han-sim	寒心	cold + mind = pathetic
결심 gyeol-ssim	決心	decide + mind = decision
진심 jin-sim	眞心	truth + mind = sincere
욕심 yok-ssim	欲心	desire + mind = greed
열심 yeol-ssim	熱心	hot + mind = diligent

Sample Sentences

의심(疑心)하지 마세요. = Don't be suspicious. / Don't doubt.

저 사람한테 관심(關心)이 많아요. = I have a lot of interest in that person.

저는 진심(眞心)이에요. = I really mean it. / I am serious.

 **필** must / without fail

 Track 43

A secret buried (丿) deep within one's heart (心) must be kept.

Character	Pronunciation	Meaning
必	필 [pil]	must, without fail, certainly

✂ Breakdown

必	心	심	heart
必	丿	별	line

Footnote
" 丿 " has no specific meaning and is used in many ways.

✏ Stroke Order

必　必　必　必　必

Examples

필요 pi-ryo	必要	certainly/must + important = need
필수 pil-ssu	必須	certainly/must + certainly/finally = mandatory, compulsory
하필 ha-pil	何必	how + certainly/must = why on earth, of all occasions
필독 pil-ttok	必讀	certainly/must + read = required reading, must-read

Sample Sentences

시간이 더 필요(必要)해요. = I need more time.

하필(何必) 오늘 비가 오네요. = Of all days, it is raining today.

이것은 필수(必須) 과목이에요. = This is a mandatory subject.

성 nature

🎵 Track 44

A person's character is shaped by what comes from (生) their heart (忄).

Character	Pronunciation	Meaning
性	성 [seong]	nature, character, sexual

✂ Breakdown

性	心/忄	심	heart
性	生	생	be born

Footnote
"生" - New sprouts (屮) start growing above ground (土), representing birth and life.

✏ Stroke Order

性 性 性 性 性 性 性 性

Examples

성격 seong-kkyeok	性格	nature/character + character/personality = personality
개성 gae-seong	個性	individual + character = individuality
성별 seong-byeol	性別	sexual + distinction = gender
이성 i-seong	理性	reign/realize/reason + nature/character = reason, rational thinking
감성 gam-seong	感性	feel + character = sensibility

Sample Sentences

두 사람은 성격(性格)이 정말 달라요. = (Those) Two people have very different personalities.

아기 성별(性別) 알아요? = Do you know the gender of the baby?

그때 제가 이성(理性)을 잃었어요. = I've lost my reason at the moment.

 애 **love**

 Track 45

"止" and "夂" are feet facing opposite directions, and between them is a heart (心) that is covered up (冖). Lovers hold (冖) their feelings in their hearts (心) and do not wish to part (止·夂).

Character	Pronunciation	Meaning
愛	애 [ae]	love

Breakdown

愛	爫→止	지	foot/stop

Footnote
An ancient pictogram shows a character that looks like a hand (爫) was modified from "foot (止)."

愛	冖	멱	cover
愛	心	심	heart
愛	夂	치	foot/walk slowly

Stroke Order

愛 愛 愛 愛 愛 愛 愛 愛
愛 愛 愛 愛 愛

Examples

애인 ae-in	愛人	love + person =	lover (boyfriend, girlfriend)
연애 yeo-nae	戀愛	love/date + love =	dating, seeing someone
애완동물 ae-wan-dong-mul	愛玩動物	love + play + animal =	pet
애정 ae-jeong	愛情	love + love =	affection

Sample Sentences

애인(愛人) 있어요? = Do you have a boyfriend/girlfriend?

1년 연애(戀愛)하고 결혼했어요. = We got married after a year of dating.

애완동물(愛玩動物) 키워요? = Do you have a pet?

 정 feeling

 Track 46

Blue water symbolizes clarity, so a blue (青) heart (忄) means one's emotions are not complicated. When one is not confused, one's 'feelings or emotions' are stronger.

Character	Pronunciation	Meaning
情	정 [jeong]	feeling, meaning, love, circumstances

Breakdown

情	心/忄	심	heart
情	青	청	blue/green

Footnote
"青" - Green rust appears (生) on red (冃→丹) metal, such as copper.

Stroke Order

情 情 情 情 情 情 情 情
情 情 情

Examples

우정 u-jeong	友情	friend + love = friendship
정보 jeong-bo	情報	meaning + inform = information
감정 gam-jeong	感情	feel + love = emotion
사정 sa-jeong	事情	matter/affair + circumstances = reason, circumstances
다정 da-jeong	多情	a lot + love = kindness, kind-heartedness
열정 yeol-jjeong	熱情	hot + love = passion
동정 dong-jeong	同情	same + feeling = sympathy
표정 pyo-jeong	表情	surface + feeling = facial expression

Sample Sentences

정보(情報)가 더 필요해요.　　= I need more information.

사정(事情)이 있었어요.　　= Something came up. / I had my reasons.

그 사람은 정말 다정(多情)해요.　　= He is very kind.

Review Quiz

1. Match the character to its sound!

ㄱ. 情 　　　　　a. 성

ㄴ. 性 　　　　　b. 정

ㄷ. 心 　　　　　c. 애

ㄹ. 愛 　　　　　d. 심

2. What does this character mean?

心　=　(　　　　　)

3. Find the character that is common among the following words and choose its English meaning.

> 必要필요　　必須필수
> 何必하필　　必讀필독

a. nature　　b. love　　c. must/without fail　　d. feeling

Answers: 1. ㄱ-b ㄴ-a ㄷ-d ㄹ-c   2. mind / heart   3. c

Flow Chart

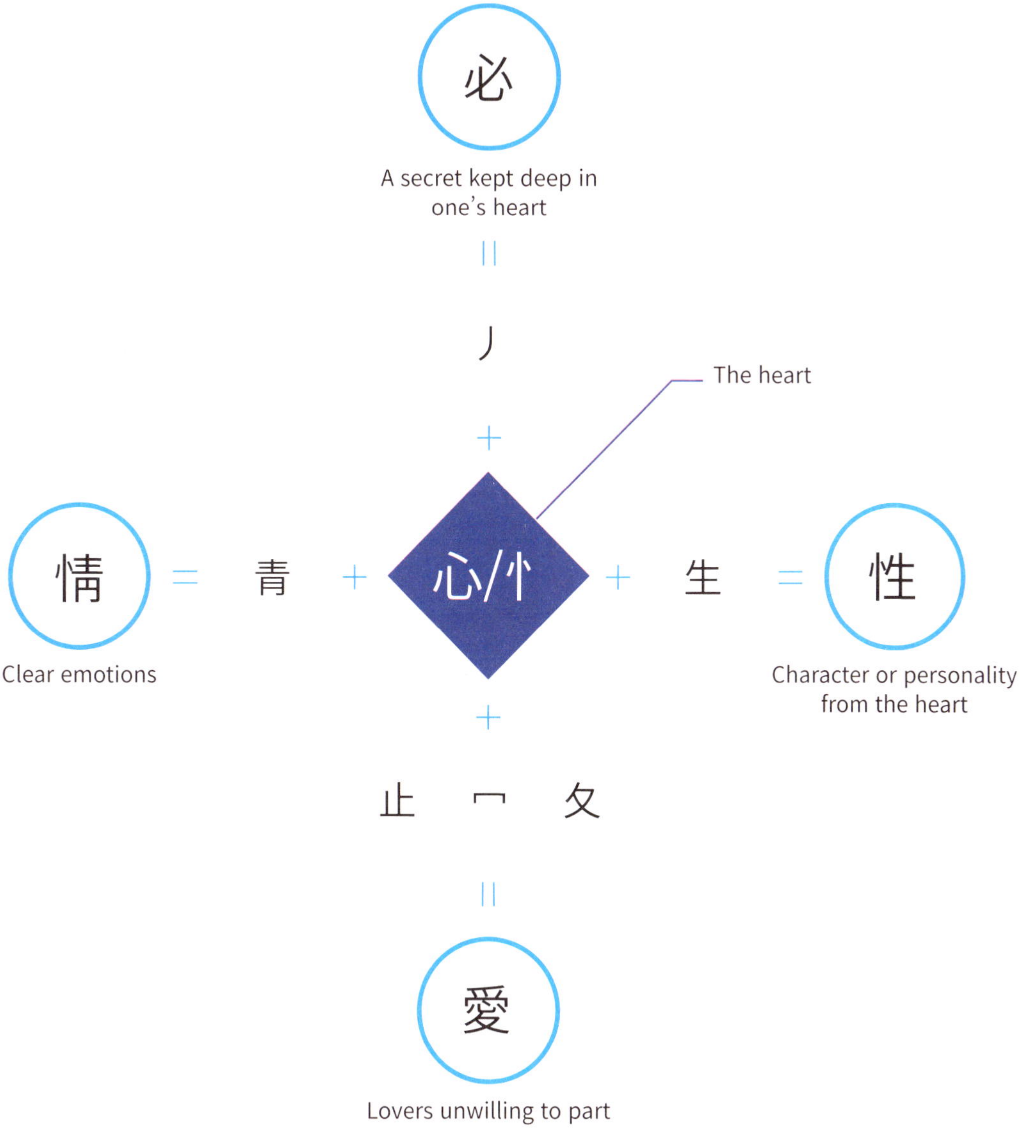

必

A secret kept deep in one's heart

‖

丿

+

心/忄 — The heart

情 = 青 + 心/忄 + 生 = 性

Clear emotions

Character or personality from the heart

+

止 冖 夂

‖

愛

Lovers unwilling to part

Learn Essential Chinese Characters Used in the Korean Language

Hanja Sadaritagi (Ghost leg) Game

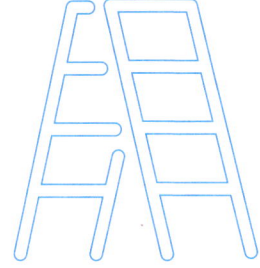

1. Choose a Chinese character from the top.

2. Trace the corresponding line down.

3. On the way down, if you come across a horizontal line, you must follow it to the adjacent vertical line on the left or the right.

4. Resume tracing down until you reach the bottom.

5. Combine your first character with the character that you land on.

6. Write the complete character in the white box below and guess the correct meaning.

Learn Essential Chinese Characters Used in the Korean Language

Hand

手 — 父 — 時 — 特 — 右 — 左 — 有 — 反 —

 수 hand

Track 47

A hand with five outstretched fingers.

Character	Pronunciation	Meaning
手	수 [su]	hand, skill, talent

Stroke Order

Examples

가수 ga-su	歌手	song + skill/talent = singer
선수 seon-su	選手	select + skill/talent = player
실수 sil-ssu	失手	lose + hand = mistake
수첩 su-cheop	手帖	hand + document = notebook

박수 bak-ssu	拍手	hit + hand = clapping
수건 su-geon	手巾	hand + towel = towel
악수 ak-ssu	握手	grasp + hand = handshake
수술 su-sul	手術	hand + skill/talent = surgery
수수료 su-su-ryo	手數料	hand + calculation + fee = commision, fee
수표 su-pyo	手票	hand + bill = check
수제 su-je	手製	hand + build = handmade, handcrafted

Sample Sentences

저는 가수(歌手)가 되고 싶어요.　　= I want to become a singer.

미안해요. 실수(失手)였어요.　　= Sorry, it was a mistake.

수건(手巾) 가져왔어요?　　= Did you bring your towel?

 부 father

 Track 48

A father holding a hammer or a stick in his hand (又) to hunt for the family.

Character	Pronunciation	Meaning
父	부 [bu]	father

 Stroke Order

Examples

부모 bu-mo	父母	father + mother = parents
부자 bu-ja	父子	father + son = father and son
부녀 bu-nyeo	父女	father + daughter = father and daughter
신부 sin-bu	神父	spirit/god + father = priest

Sample Sentences

부모(父母)님 선물 샀어요? = Did you buy presents for your parents?

부녀(父女)가 20년 만에 만났어요. = The father and the daughter met for the first time in 20 years.

신부(神父)님이 많이 도와주셨어요. = The priest helped me a lot.

 시 time

 Track 49

This character tells us that the local office (寺) used to ring a bell to tell people the time, based on the sun (日) dial.

Character	Pronunciation	Meaning
時	시 [si]	time

 Breakdown

時	日	일	sun
時	寺	사	government office/ Buddhist temple

Footnote
To serve on one's feet (土→止) and hands (寸). At first it was used to describe an office of the king, but it became "temple 寺" after Buddhism was brought into China.

Stroke Order

時 時 時 時 時 時 時 時 時 時

Examples

시간 si-gan	時間	time + gap = time
시간표 si-gan-pyo	時間表	time + gap + diagram/table = timetable
시대 si-dae	時代	time + time = era
잠시 jam-si	暫時	short moment + time = short while
즉시 jeuk-ssi	卽時	soon/now + time = immediately
시계 si-gye	時計	time + calculate = clock, watch
임시 im-si	臨時	temporary + time = temporary
당시 dang-si	當時	this/that + time = at that time

Sample Sentences

지금 시간(時間) 있어요?   = Do you have time now?

잠시(暫時)만요.   = Just a second.

시계(時計)가 없어요.   = I don't have a clock/watch.

特 특 special

 Track 50

Buddhists do not kill animals or eat meat. When a bull (牛) is offered to a Buddhist temple (寺), it is considered a special offering.

Character	Pronunciation	Meaning
特	특 [teuk]	special

✂ Breakdown

特	牛	우	cow
特	寺	사	Buddhist temple

✏ Stroke Order

特 特 特 特 特 特 特 特 特 特

Examples

특별 teuk-ppyeol	特別	special + different = special
특징 teuk-jjing	特徵	special + call = characteristic, feature
특집 teuk-jjip	特輯	special + gather = special edition, special episode
독특 dok-teuk	獨特	alone + special = unique
특강 teuk-kkang	特講	special + learn = special lecture
특권 teuk-kkwon	特權	special + power = privilege
특기 teuk-kki	特技	special + talent = specialty
기특 gi-teuk	奇特	commendable + special = commendable, praiseworthy

Sample Sentences

오늘은 특별(特別)한 날이에요. = Today is a special day.

여름 방학에 한국어 특강(特講)을 들었어요. = I attended a special lecture on the Korean language during summer vacation.

제 딸이 정말 기특(奇特)해요. = My daughter is really commendable/praiseworthy.

Review Quiz

1. Match the character to its sound!

ㄱ. 特   a. 시

ㄴ. 時   b. 수

ㄷ. 手   c. 특

2. What does this character mean?

手　=　(　　　　　)

3. Find the character that is common among the following words and choose its English meaning.

> 父母부모　　父子부자
> 父女부녀　　神父신부

a. special　　b. time　　c. father　　d. hand

Answers:　1. ㄱ - c ㄴ - a ㄷ - b　2. hand　3. c

Flow Chart

手 ···· compare ···· 父

An open hand　　　　　　　Holding an ax

compare

촌
Joint
Hand and finger joints

寸

+

止 — 지
Feet standing still

=

特 = 牛 + 寺 + 日 = 時

Bull offered to　　　To serve Buddha　　　The government office
a temple　　　　　　　　　　　　　　　　ringing a bell to signal
　　　　　　　　　　　　　　　　　　　　the time

Learn Essential Chinese Characters Used in the Korean Language　　　141

 우 right

 Track 51

The hand (ナ) that helps the mouth (口). In other words, the 'right' hand used to eat. Of course, some people are left-handed, but in China most people use chopsticks with their right hand.

Character	Pronunciation	Meaning
右	우 [u]	right

✂ Breakdown

右	ナ→又	우	hand/again

Footnote
When "又" was first created, it meant 'right hand', but because people used their hands to do chores again and again, it came to mean 'again.' When used as part of a more complicated character, it's better to think of the meaning as 'hand.'

右	口	구	mouth

✏ Stroke Order

右 右 右 右 右

Your First Hanja Guide

Examples

우측
u-cheuk

右側

right + side = the right side, one's right

우회전
u-hoe-jeon

右廻轉

right + turn + roll = right turn

Sample Sentences

우측(右側)으로 옮겨 주세요. = Please move it to the right side.

 좌 left

 Track 52

A hand (ナ) holding a tool (工). It means 'left' because that's the hand that holds the tool to help the right hand do the work.

Character	Pronunciation	Meaning
左	좌 [jwa]	left

✂ **Breakdown**

左	ナ→又	우	hand/again
左	工	공	tool/work

✏ **Stroke Order**

左　左　左　左　左

Examples

좌측 左側 left + side = the left side, one's left
jwa-cheuk

좌회전 左廻轉 left + turn + roll = left turn
jwa-hoe-jeon

Sample Sentences

좌측(左側)에 있는 문으로 들어오세요. = Please come in through the door on the left.

 유 have / exist

 Track 53

A hand (ナ) holding meat (肉), which is a sacrifice. It came to mean 'have or exist.'

Character	Pronunciation	Meaning
有	유 [yu]	have, exist

 Breakdown

| 有 | ナ→又 | 우 | hand/again |
| 有 | 月→肉 | 육 | meat |

Footnote
"Moon 月" can also mean "meat 肉" when used as part of another character.

Stroke Order

有　有　有　有　有　有

Examples

유명 yu-myeong	有名	exist/have + name	= famous
공유 gong-yu	共有	together + exist/have	= share
고유 go-yu	固有	originally/from the first + exist/have	= inherent, characteristic
유죄 yu-joe	有罪	exist/have + fault	= guilty

Sample Sentences

저 가수 유명(有名)해요? = Is that singer famous?

이거 공유(共有)해도 돼요? = Can I share this?

한국의 고유(固有) 음식이에요. = It's a Korean traditional food.

 **반** opposite

 Track 54

To put one's hand (又) against a cliff (厂) to overcome and oppose an obstacle.

Character	Pronunciation	Meaning
反	반 [ban]	opposite, return

Examples

반대 ban-dae	反對	opposite + face/look at = opposition, objection
반성 ban-seong	反省	return + realize = repent, self-remorse
반응 ba-neung	反應	return + accept/answer = reaction
반복 ban-bok	反復	return + return/repeat = repetition
반항 ba-nang	反抗	opposite + compete/resist = defiance
반칙 ban-chik	反則	opposite + rule = foul, rule violation, cheating
반전 ban-jeon	反轉	opposite + roll = reversal, plot twist
반사 ban-sa	反射	return + shine = reflection

Sample Sentences

그 사람 의견에 반대(反對)합니다.　　= I object to his opinion.

제 과거를 반성(反省)하고 있어요.　　= I am repenting on my past.

왜 같은 말을 반복(反復)해요?　　= Why do you repeat the same words?

Review Quiz

1. Match the character to its sound!

ㄱ. 左	a. 반

ㄴ. 右	b. 우

ㄷ. 反	c. 좌

2. What does this character mean?

右 = (   )

3. Find the character that is common among the following words and choose its English meaning.

有名유명   有罪유죄   共有공유   固有고유

a. return   b. left/right   c. have/exist   d. opposite

Answers: 1. ㄱ-c ㄴ-b ㄷ-a   2. right   3. c

Flow Chart

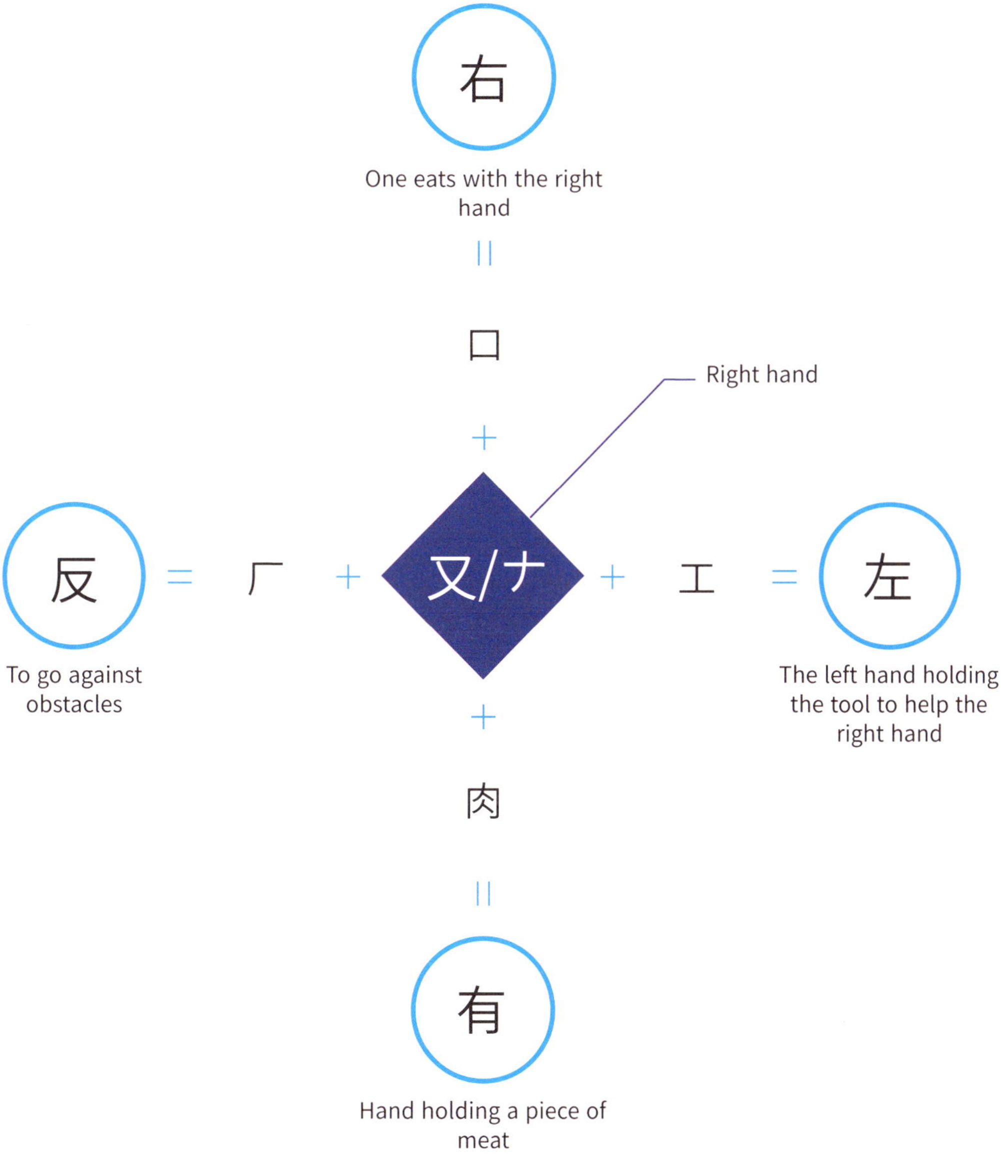

右
One eats with the right hand

‖

口

+

反 = 厂 + 又/ナ + 工 = 左

Right hand

To go against obstacles

The left hand holding the tool to help the right hand

+

肉

‖

有

Hand holding a piece of meat

Learn Essential Chinese Characters Used in the Korean Language

Foot

足 — 出 — 正 — 題 — 夏 — 後 —
冬 — 行 — 運 — 道 — 通 —

 foot

 Track 55

This character means 'foot', but it also refers to the shin, calf, ankle, and foot.

Character	Pronunciation	Meaning
足	족 [jok]	foot, enough

✏️ Stroke Order

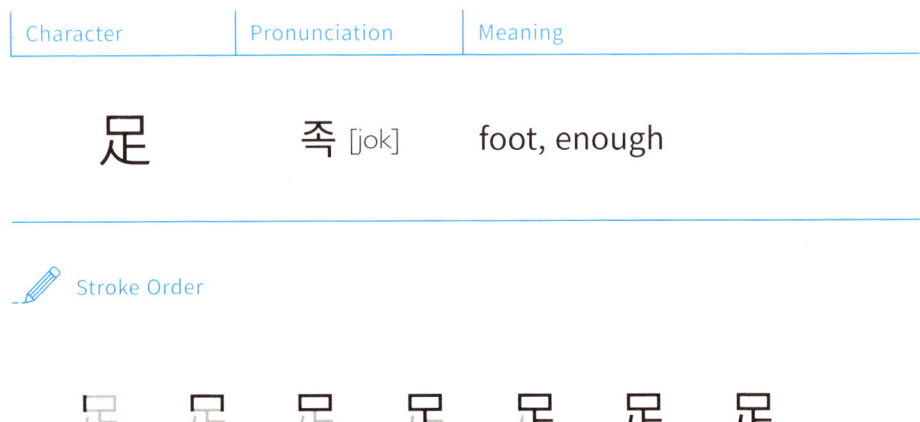

Examples

부족 bu-jok	不足	not + enough =	shortage
만족 man-jok	滿足	full + enough =	satisfaction
불만족 bul-man-jok	不滿足	not + full + enough =	dissatisfaction
충족 chung-jok	充足	fill + enough =	satisfy
풍족 pung-jok	豊足	rich year/well-to-do + enough =	affluence

Sample Sentences

시간이 너무 부족(不足)해요.   = I have such a shortage of time.

이 결과에 만족(滿足)해요.   = I am satisfied with this result.

 출 go out

 Track 56

According to ancient Chinese texts, this represents feet (止) walking out of a hut (凵).

Character	Pronunciation	Meaning
出	출 [chul]	go out, be born

Breakdown

出	止	지	foot/stop

Footnote
"止" represents the shape of a foot that is waiting to move, but because it is not moving at the moment, it also means 'stop.'

出	凵	감	hut

Stroke Order

屮 屮 屮 出 出

Examples

출구 chul-gu	出口	go out + mouth/door =	exit
출입문 chu-rim-mun	出入門	go out + enter + door =	gate
외출 oe-chul	外出	outside + go out =	going out, outing
출발 chul-bal	出發	go out + shoot/leave =	departure
탈출 tal-chul	脫出	get out (of) + go out =	escape
출장 chul-jjang	出張	go out + do/have =	business trip
출신 chul-ssin	出身	be born + body =	origin
출근 chul-geun	出勤	go out + diligent/work =	going to work
출석 chul-sseok	出席	go out + seat =	attendance
가출 ga-chul	家出	house + go out =	running away from home

Sample Sentences

왼쪽에 출입문(出入門)이 있어요.　　= The gate is on the left.

지금 출발(出發)할 거예요.　　= We are going to depart now.

출장(出張) 언제 가요?　　= When are you going on your business trip?

 정 **right / correct**

Track 57

This character describes the feet (止) of soldiers going off to attack the enemy (一), and means 'to conquer.' To do so is the 'right' thing.

Character	Pronunciation	Meaning
正	정 [jeong]	right, correct, proper

✂ Breakdown

正	一		symbol	enemy camp
正	止	지	foot/stop

Sidenote

Ancient Chinese texts show 'feet (止) facing a castle (口).'

✏ Stroke Order

正 正 正 正 正

Examples

정확 jeong-hwak	正確	right + definite = accurate
정직 jeong-jik	正直	right + straight/upright = honesty
수정 su-jeong	修正	repair + right = modification
정상 jeong-sang	正常	right + ordinary/always = normal
정답 jeong-dap	正答	right + answer = correct answer

Sample Sentences

우리 반에서 제일 정직(正直)한 학생이에요.

= He is the most honest student in our class.

약간의 수정(修正)이 필요해요.

= It needs a bit of modification.

이 문제는 정답(正答)이 없어요.

= This question has no right answer.

제 subject

Track 58

To be able to tell the contents of a book accurately (是), the subject is written at the head (頁), or in the front.

Character	Pronunciation	Meaning
題	제 [je]	subject, title, question

✂ Breakdown

題	是	시	correct

Footnote
"是" - Feet heading out to conquer (正) are facing the sun (日). To head towards the light means it is the right thing to do.

題	頁	혈	head

✏ Stroke Order

題 題 題 題 題 題 題 題 題
題 題 題 題 題 題 題 題 題

Examples

제목
je-mok
題目
title/subject + eye/title = title

문제
mun-je
問題
ask + question = question, problem

숙제
suk-jje
宿題
sleep/accommodation + question = homework

주제
ju-je
主題
most major/most basic + title/subject = subject, topic

Sample Sentences

이 영화 제목(題目)이 뭐예요?   = What is the title of this movie?

시험 문제(問題)가 너무 어려워요.   = The exam questions are too difficult.

숙제(宿題)가 정말 많아요.   = I have so much homework.

Review Quiz

1. Match the character to its sound!

ㄱ. 題　　　　　　　　a. 제

ㄴ. 正　　　　　　　　b. 출

ㄷ. 出　　　　　　　　c. 정

2. What does this character mean?

足　＝　(　　　　　　)

3. Find the character that is common among the following words and choose its English meaning.

> 出口출구　　出入門출입문
> 外出외출　　出發출발

　a. subject　　b. question　　c. right/correct　　d. go out

Answers:　　1. ㄱ - a   ㄴ - c   ㄷ - b　　2. foot　　3. d

Flow Chart

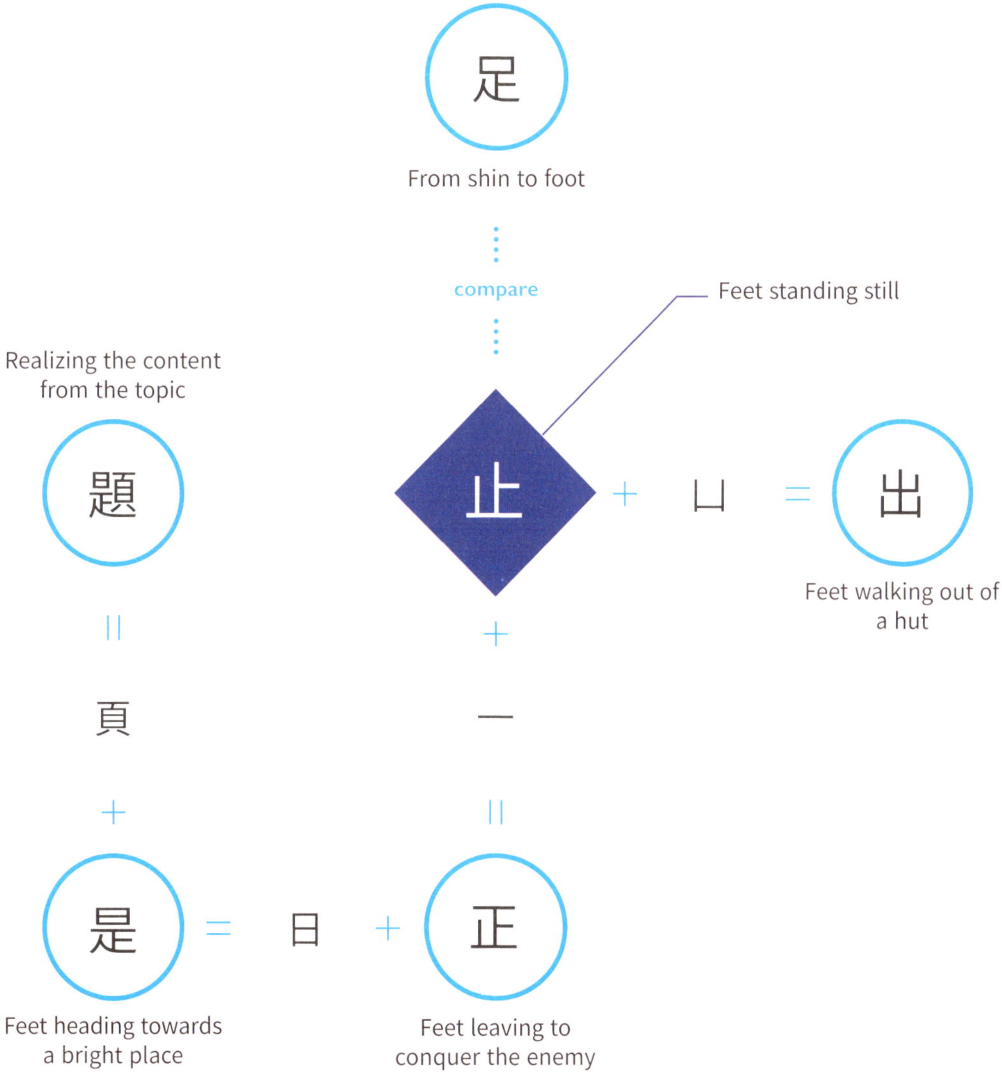

足
From shin to foot

⋮
compare
⋮

止 — Feet standing still

題 + 口 = 出

Realizing the content from the topic

∥

頁

+

—

∥

是 = 日 + 正

Feet walking out of a hut

Feet heading towards a bright place

Feet leaving to conquer the enemy

Learn Essential Chinese Characters Used in the Korean Language

 하 summer

 Track 59

Some say this character describes a shaman (頁) with wildly dancing feet (夂). The ritual for rain was the most important (sacrificial) ritual, and since the rain mostly came during the summer, this character came to mean 'summer' during the Eastern Zhou Dynasty (东周, 770~256 BC).

Character	Pronunciation	Meaning
夏	하 [ha]	summer

Breakdown

夏	頁	혈	head
夏	夂	치	foot/walk slowly

Footnote
"夂" - Upside-down feet (止) because someone pulled a man down from behind. When one is being stopped from walking at normal speed, one has to 'walk slowly or fall behind others.'

Stroke Order

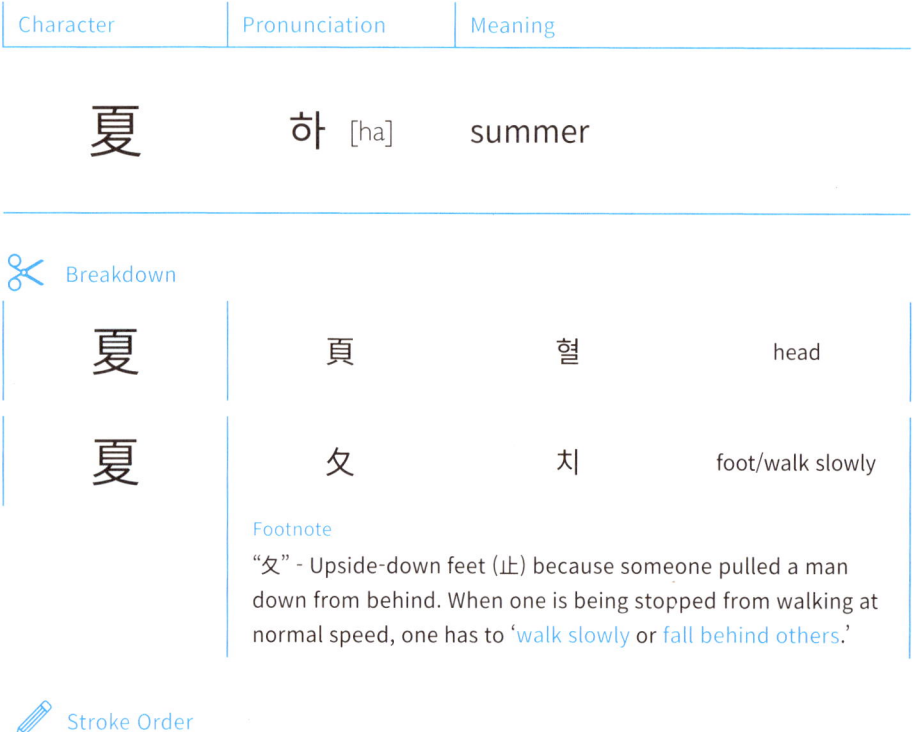

Examples

하복 夏服 summer + clothing/apparel = summer clothing
ha-bok   (usually in school)

Sample Sentences

우리 교복은 하복(夏服)이 더 예뻐요. = The summer uniform for our school is prettier (than the winter uniform).

 back / after

 Track 60

Prisoners walking (彳) in single file with their feet (夂) bound by a long rope (糸). Because people with feet tied up (糸) can only walk (彳) slowly (夂), this character came to mean 'behind, next, later or in the back.'

Character	Pronunciation	Meaning
後	후 [hu]	back, after, rear

✂ Breakdown

後	彳	척	walk
後	幺 → 糸	사	thread/rope
後	夂	치	foot/walk slowly

✏ Stroke Order

後 後 後 後 後 後 後 後 後

Examples

오후 o-hu	午後	noon + after = afternoon
후회 hu-hoe	後悔	after + regret = regret
후원 hu-won	後援	back + help = sponsorship
후원자 hu-won-ja	後援者	back + help + person = sponsor
후원금 hu-won-geum	後援金	back + help + money = donation
후문 hu-mun	後門	back + door = back gate, rumor
후유증 hu-yu-jjeung	後遺症	after + leave/remain + symptom = aftermath, consequences
후배 hu-bae	後輩	after + group = junior
후진 hu-jin	後進	back + go forward = reversing, backing up (the car)

Sample Sentences

오후(午後)에 비가 왔어요. = It rained in the afternoon.

후원금(後援金)을 받았어요. = We received a donation.

요즘 후유증(後遺症)을 앓고 있어요. = I am experiencing the consequences these days.

 winter

 Track 61

In the bitter cold (冫) of winter, people tend to curl up and walk slowly (夂).

Character	Pronunciation	Meaning
冬	동 [dong]	winter

✂ Breakdown

冬	夂	치	walk slowly
冬	冫	빙	ice

Sidenote

Its ancient character is an image of knots made at both ends of a thread. It describes 'winter' because everything ends its growth during winter.

✏ Stroke Order

Examples

동복
dong-bok

冬服

winter + clothing/apparel = winter clothing (usually in school)

Sample Sentences

오늘 동복(冬服)을 입고 학교에 갔어요.

= Today, I went to school wearing my winter uniform.

Review Quiz

1. Match the character to its sound!

ㄱ. 夏   a. 하

ㄴ. 冬   b. 동

2. What does this character mean?

冬 = (   )

3. Find the character that is common among the following words and choose its English meaning.

午後오후   後悔후회
後援者후원자   後進후진

a. morning   b. uniform   c. back/after   d. season

Answers: 1. ㄱ - a ㄴ - b   2. winter   3. c

Flow Chart

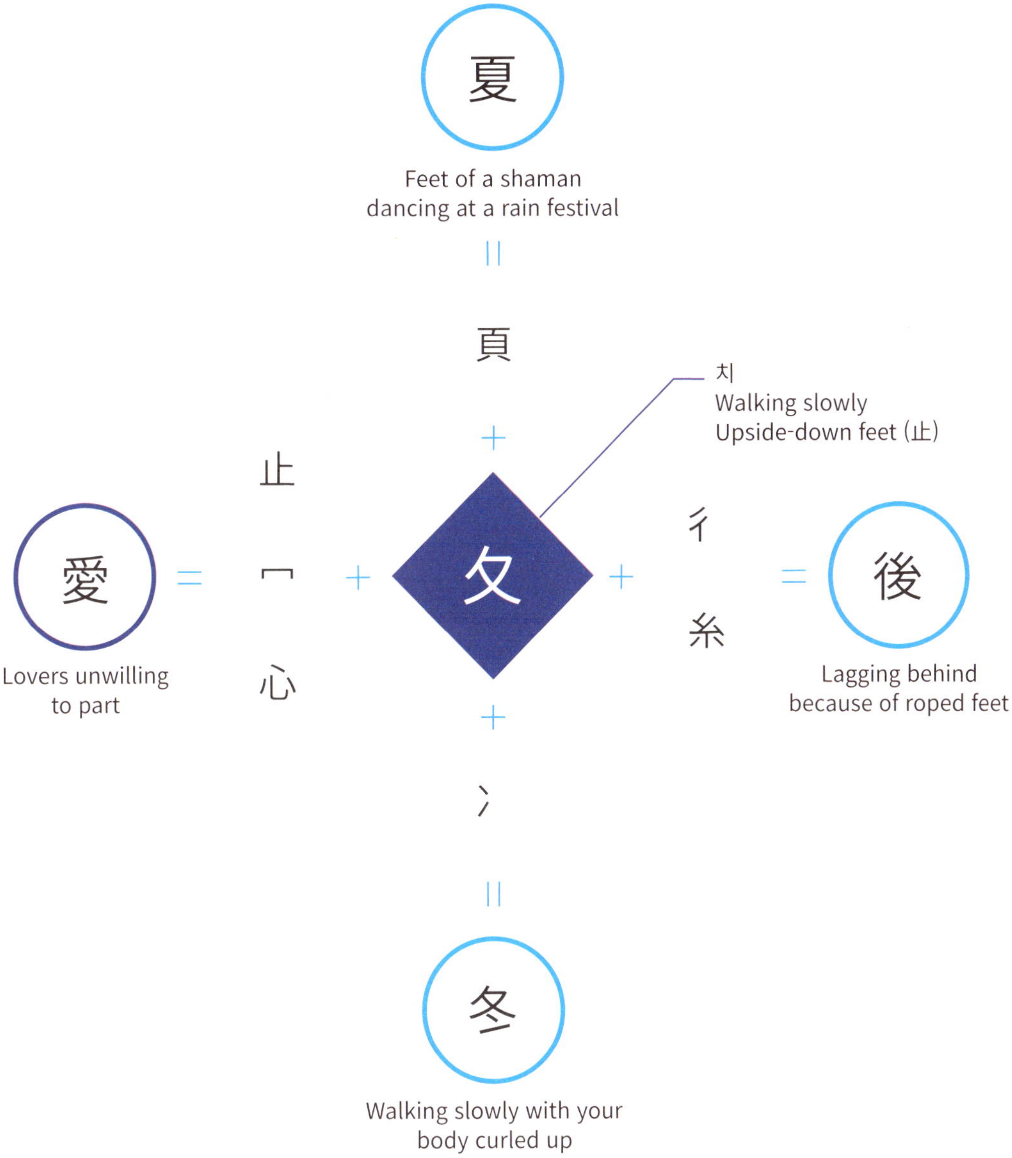

夏
Feet of a shaman dancing at a rain festival

頁
+

치
Walking slowly
Upside-down feet (止)

愛 = 止 ㄇ 心 + 夂 + 彳 糸 = 後

Lovers unwilling to part

Lagging behind because of roped feet

+
冫
=
冬
Walking slowly with your body curled up

Learn Essential Chinese Characters Used in the Korean Language

 행 go

 Track 62

Taking the shape of a crossroad, this character means 'to go or walk.'

Character	Pronunciation	Meaning
行	행 [haeng]	go

✂ Breakdown

| 行 | 彳 | 척 | walk |
| 行 | 亍 | 촉 | walk with a limp |

Sidenote

"彳" is the left side of the crossroad, while "亍" is the right side. Neither character (彳, 亍) can be used on its own.

✏ Stroke Order

172　　　Your First Hanja Guide

Examples

여행 yeo-haeng	旅行	traveler + go = travel
여행사 yeo-haeng-sa	旅行社	travel + company = travel agency
비행기 bi-haeng-gi	飛行機	fly + go + machine = airplane
은행 eu-naeng	銀行	silver + go = bank
행사 haeng-sa	行事	go + affair = event
유행 yu-haeng	流行	flow + go = trend
운행 u-naeng	運行	drive + go = running/operating a vehicle
행동 haeng-dong	行動	go + move = action
급행 geu-paeng	急行	urgent + go = rush

Sample Sentences

여행(旅行) 가고 싶어요.   = I want to travel.

비행기(飛行機) 타면 1시간 걸려요.   = It takes one hour by airplane.

급행(急行) 열차 타면 금방 가요.   = If you take the express train, you get there quickly.

 운 **move / transfer**

 **Track 63**

An image of a wagon (車) carrying (辶) munitions covered (冖) with cloth so that it cannot be seen.

Character	Pronunciation	Meaning
運	운 [un]	move, transfer, luck, carry

 Breakdown

運	冖	멱	cover
運	車	차/거	wagon
運	辶	착	go

Sidenote

"Army, 軍" represents the image of military supplies in a wagon (車) covered (冖) by a cloth to be taken far away for war.

Stroke Order

Examples

운동 un-dong	運動	move + move = exercise
운동장 un-dong-jang	運動場	move + move + yard = schoolyard
행운 haeng-un	幸運	lucky + luck = good luck
운전 un-jeon	運轉	move + roll = drive
운전면허 un-jeon-myeo-neo	運轉免許	move + roll + license = driver's license
운명 un-myeong	運命	luck + life = fate
기운 gi-un	氣運	atmosphere/air + move = energy, stamina
운세 un-se	運勢	luck + situation = fortune

Sample Sentences

저는 매일 아침에 운동(運動)을 해요. = I work out every morning.

드디어 운전면허(運轉免許)를 땄어요. = I finally got my driver's license.

요즘 기운(氣運)이 없어요. = I have no energy these days.

도 way / morals

Track 64

The direction that the head (首), or the leader goes (辶), is the way his men must follow. This character also means morals, because it's the way one must go, the right way.

Character	Pronunciation	Meaning
道	도 [do]	way, morals

Breakdown

道	首	수	head
道	辶	착	go

Footnote

"辶" - Ancient Chinese texts show a combination of "行 crossroad" and "止 foot", which means 'a road describing distance', or 'to go.'

Stroke Order

道 道 道 道 道 道 道 道
道 道 道 道 道

Examples

도로 do-ro	道路	way + street =	road
도덕 do-deok	道德	morals + virtue =	morality, ethics
복도 bok-tto	複道	overlap + way =	corridor
효도 hyo-do	孝道	filial + morals =	filial piety

Sample Sentences

고속 도로(道路)에 차가 많아요. = There are many cars on the expressway.

복도(複道) 끝에 화장실이 있어요. = The restroom is at the end of the corridor.

부모님께 효도(孝道)하세요. = Be filial to your parents.

 통 **pass through**

Track 65

Wind can pass through (辶) the holes of a mesh basket (甬).

Character	Pronunciation	Meaning
通	행 [tong]	pass through

✂ Breakdown

通	甬	동	(bamboo) tube

Footnote
"甬" - A mesh bag (用) with a handle (⌐) shaped like a tube.

通	辶	착	go

✎ Stroke Order

通 通 通 通 通 通 通 通
通 通 通

Examples

보통 bo-tong	普通	wide + pass through = normal
교통 gyo-tong	交通	come and go/exchange + pass through = traffic
통과 tong-gwa	通過	pass through + pass/go by = pass
통장 tong-jang	通帳	pass through + ledger/books = bankbook
통화 tong-hwa	通話	pass through + word = phone call
통역 tong-yeok	通譯	pass through + translate = translation, interpretation
소통 so-tong	疏通	communicate + pass through = communication
공통점 gong-tong-jjeom	共通點	same/shared + pass through + point = common ground

Sample Sentences

보통(普通) 몇 시에 학교에 가요? = What time do you normally go to school?

오늘 은행에서 통장(通帳)을 하나 만들었어요. = I made a bankbook at the bank today.

우리 부부는 공통점(共通點)이 많아요. = My spouse and I have a lot in common.

Review Quiz

1. Match the character to its sound!

   ㄱ. 道　　　　　　　　a. 도

   ㄴ. 運　　　　　　　　b. 행

   ㄷ. 行　　　　　　　　c. 운

2. What does this character mean?

   道　＝　(　　　　　)

3. Find the character that is common among the following words and choose its English meaning.

   通過통과　　通譯통역
   疏通소통　　通話통화

   a. go　　b. pass through　　c. move　　d. luck

Answers: 1. ㄱ - a ㄴ - c ㄷ - b　 2. way / morals　 3. b

Flow Chart

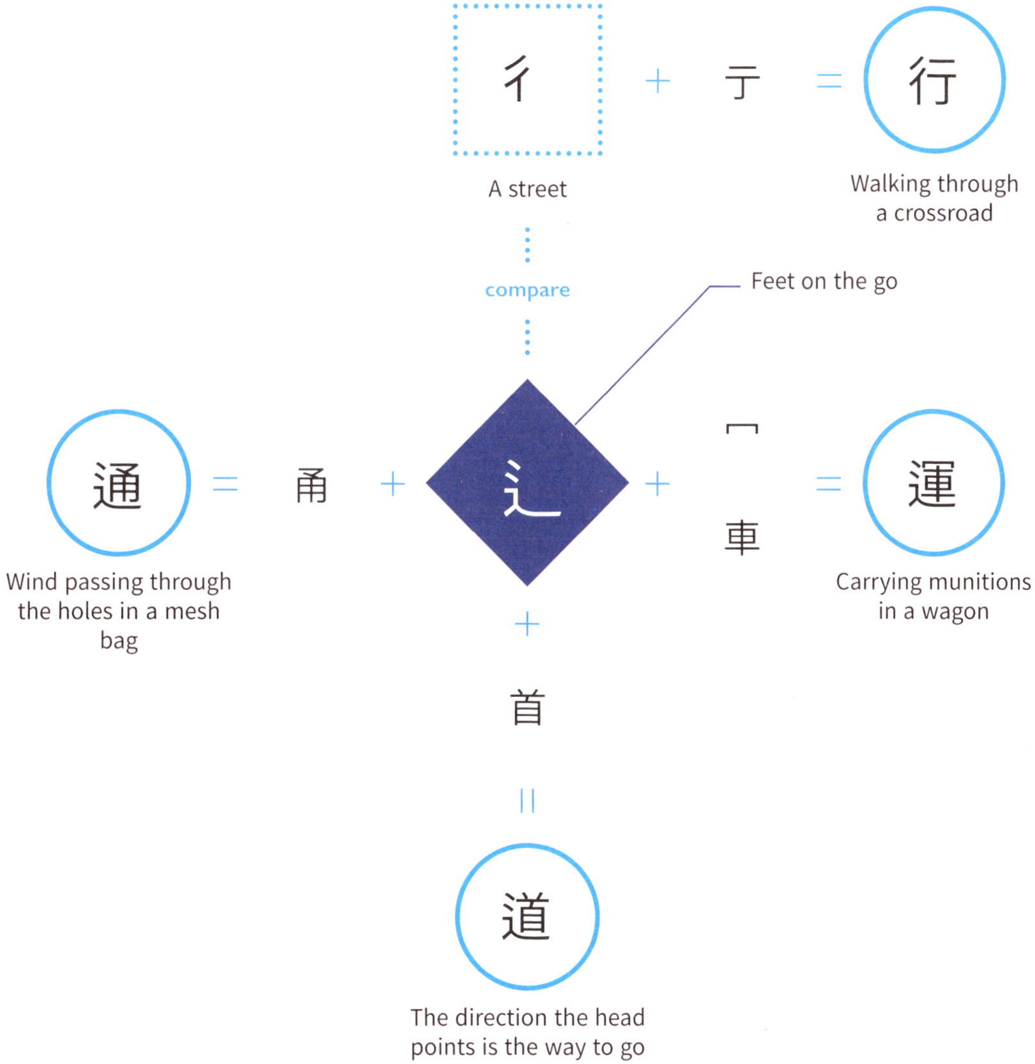

彳 + 亍 = 行

彳 A street

行 Walking through a crossroad

compare

Feet on the go

通 = 甬 + 辶 + 车 = 運

通 Wind passing through the holes in a mesh bag

運 Carrying munitions in a wagon

+ 首 = 道

道 The direction the head points is the way to go

Learn Essential Chinese Characters Used in the Korean Language

Shelter

家 — 安 — 室 — 門 — 問 —
間 — 內 — 南 — 市 — 雨 —

 house / -ist

 Track 66

Combination of house (宀) and pig (豕), which gives birth to many babies, so the character came to mean a *family*. It is a play on words for fertility. Used also as an ending for someone in a specific profession, like "*-ist*" in pianist.

Character	Pronunciation	Meaning
家	가 [ga]	house, -ist, family

✂ Breakdown

家	宀	면	house

Footnote
"宀" - A *house*, represented by its roof. When part of another character, it gives the meaning of a *house* where people live.

家	豕	시	pig

 Stroke Order

Examples

가족 ga-jok	家族	house + people = family
작가 jak-kka	作家	make + -ist = author
화가 hwa-ga	畵家	painting + -ist = painter
가난 ga-nan	家難	house/family + difficult = poverty
가장 ga-jang	家長	house/family + adult/leader = breadwinner
가구 ga-gu	家具	house + organize/tool = furniture
국가 guk-kka	國家	country + house = nation
전문가 jeon-mun-ga	專門家	only + field + -ist = expert

Sample Sentences

우리 가족(家族)은 다섯 명이에요.   = My family consists of 5 people.

어렸을 때 정말 가난(家難)했어요.   = I was really poor when I was little.

어제 가구(家具)를 샀어요.   = I bought furniture yesterday.

 안 peaceful

 Track 67

In traditional Chinese culture, a peaceful family meant the woman (女) stayed at home (宀) to take care of the family.

Character	Pronunciation	Meaning
安	안 [ga]	peaceful, comfortable

Breakdown

安	宀	면	house
安	女	녀	woman

Stroke Order

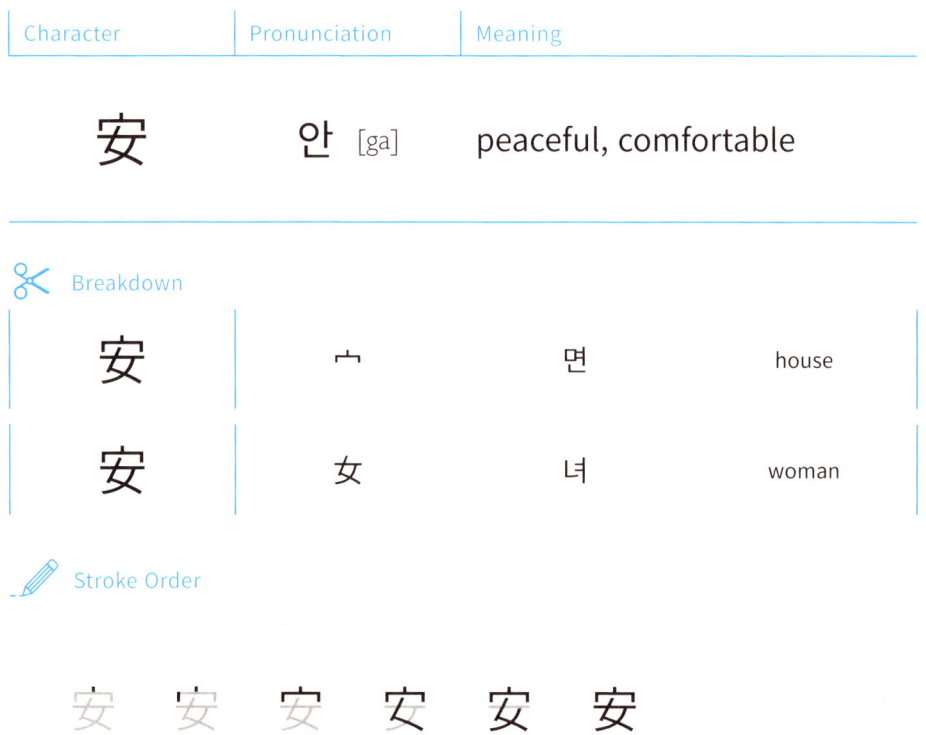

186   Your First Hanja Guide

Examples

안전 an-jeon	安全	comfortable + completely = safe
불안 bu-ran	不安	not + peaceful = anxiety
편안 pyeo-nan	便安	comfortable + comfortable = comfortable
안부 an-bu	安否	peaceful + not = inquire about someone, ask whether someone is well or not
안정 an-jeong	安定	peaceful + decide/fix = stability

Sample Sentences

이곳은 안전(安全)해요. = This place is safe.

이 소파 정말 편안(便安)해요. = This couch is really comfortable.

할머니한테 안부(安否) 전해 주세요. = Please say hi to your grandmother for me.

  room

It was tradition to shoot a sacred arrow, and build a house (宀) with many rooms wherever it landed (至).

Character	Pronunciation	Meaning
室	실 [sil]	room, house

✂ Breakdown

室	宀	면	house
室	至	지	arrive

Footnote
"至" - An arrow (矢) that has been shot into the ground (土) has reached its target. In ancient days, a sacred arrow (矢) was shot and where it landed (一) was where they built important buildings or temples.

✎ Stroke Order

室 室 室 室 室 室 室 室 室

Examples

교실 gyo-sil	敎室	teach + room = classroom
화장실 hwa-jang-sil	化粧室	become + decorate + room = bathroom
사무실 sa-mu-sil	事務室	work + task + room = office
실내 sil-lae	室內	house + inside = indoor
실외 si-roe	室外	house + outside = outdoor
휴게실 hyu-ge-sil	休偈室	rest + rest + room = lounge
회의실 hoe-ui-sil	會議室	gather + discuss + room = conference room

Sample Sentences

여기는 3학년 교실(敎室)이에요. = This is a classroom for third-year students.

집 근처에 사무실(事務室)이 있어요. = My office is near my house.

휴게실(休偈室)에 사람이 많아요. = There are a lot of people in the lounge.

Review Quiz

1. Match the character to its sound!

ㄱ. 安　　　　　　　　　a. 안

ㄴ. 家　　　　　　　　　b. 가

2. What does this character mean?

家　＝　(　　　　　)

3. Find the character that is common among the following words and choose its English meaning.

> 教室교실　　化粧室화장실
> 會議室회의실　　事務室사무실

a. room　　b. peaceful　　c. comfortable　　d. safe

Answers:　1. ㄱ - a　ㄴ - b　2. house / -ist　3. a

Flow Chart

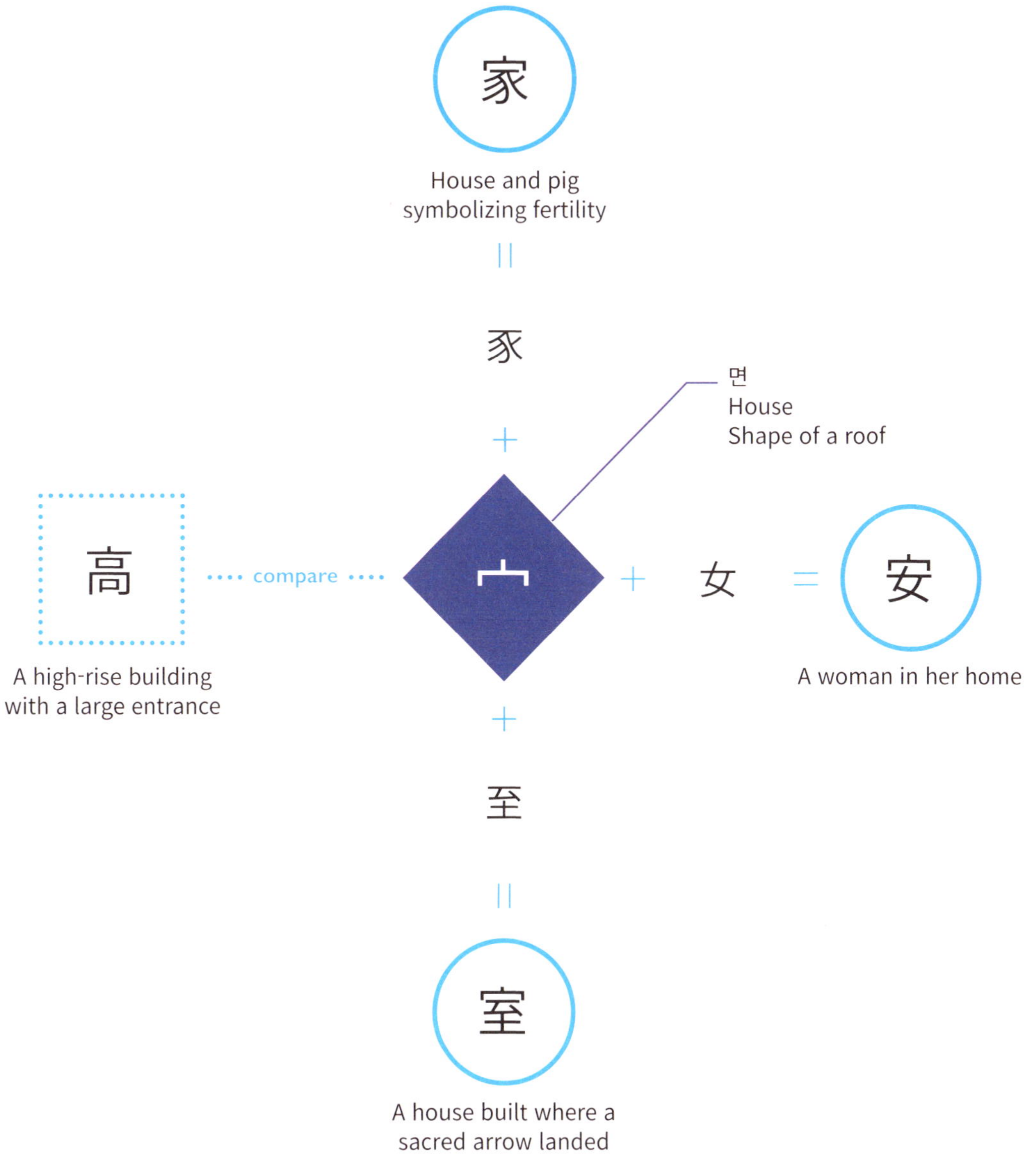

家
House and pig symbolizing fertility

=

豕

+

면
House
Shape of a roof

高 ···· compare ···· 宀 + 女 = 安

A high-rise building with a large entrance

A woman in her home

+

至

=

室

A house built where a sacred arrow landed

 문 door / gate

 Track 69

Palaces and large houses had doors that came in a set of two.

Character	Pronunciation	Meaning
門	문 [mun]	door

Stroke Order

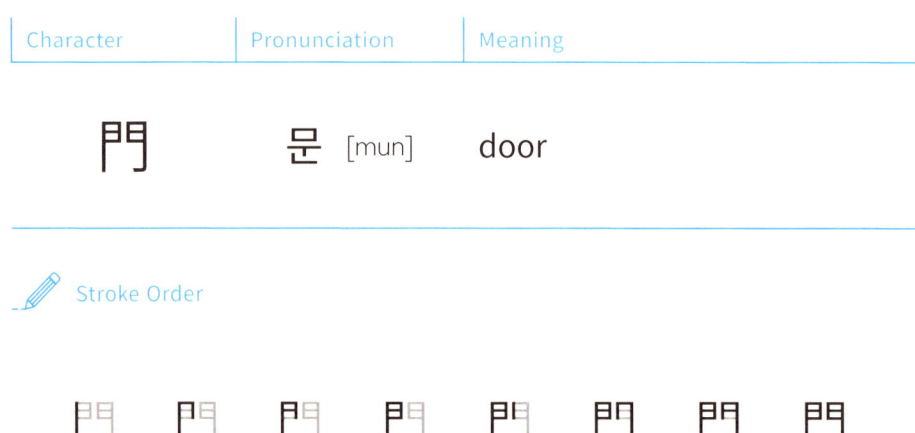

Examples

창문 chang-mun	窓門	window + door =	window
정문 jeong-mun	正門	right/upright + door =	front door
후문 hu-mun	後門	back + door =	back door
입문 im-mun	入門	go in + door =	introduction (to a field of study)

Sample Sentences

창문(窓門) 좀 열어 줄래요? = Will you open the window?

우리 정문(正門)에서 만나요. = Let's meet at the front door.

후문(後門)으로 나가면 가게가 있어요. = If you go out the back door, there is a store.

 문 ask

Track 70

To open a door (門) and ask (口) if one is at the right house.

Character	Pronunciation	Meaning
問	문 [mun]	ask

Breakdown

問	門	문	door
問	口	구	mouth

Stroke Order

問 問 問 問 問 問 問 問
問 問 問

Examples

문제 mun-je	問題	ask + title	= question, problem
방문 bang-mun	訪問	find + ask	= visit
학문 hang-mun	學問	learn + ask	= study
질문 jil-mun	質問	foundation/nature + ask	= question
문병 mun-byeong	問病	ask + sick	= visiting a sick person
문의 mu-nui	問議	ask + discuss	= inquire

Sample Sentences

회사에 문제(問題)가 생겼어요.
= We have a problem at our company.

질문(質問) 있어요?
= Do you have a question?

친구가 아파서 문병(問甁)을 갔어요.
= My friend was sick, so I went to visit her in the hospital.

 간 interval / between

 Track 71

This describes the sun (日) shining through a space in the door (門). It also came to mean 'room', the space between two walls.

Character	Pronunciation	Meaning
間	간 [gan]	interval, between, gap, while

✂ Breakdown

間	門	문	door
間	日	일	sun

✏ Stroke Order

間 間 間 間 間 間 間 間
間 間 間 間

Examples

한글	漢字	의미
시간 si-gan	時間	time + gap = time
순간 sun-gan	瞬間	blink + while = moment
기간 gi-gan	期間	period + while = period, term
간격 gan-gyeok	間隔	gap + leave space = interval, space
인간 in-gan	人間	person + between = human
중간 jung-gan	中間	middle + between = middle
야간 ya-gan	夜間	night + while = night, the night time

Sample Sentences

지금 시간(時間) 있어요? = Do you have time now?

다음 주가 시험 기간(期間)이에요. = My exam period is next week.

우리 학교랑 집 중간(中間)에서 만나요. = Let's meet halfway between school and home.

Review Quiz

1. Match the character to its sound!

ㄱ. 間   a. 문

ㄴ. 門   b. 간

2. What does this character mean?

門   =   (   )

3. Find the character that is common among the following words and choose its English meaning.

| 問題문제   問議문의 |
| 質問질문   學問학문 |

a. ask   b. answer   c. interval/between   d. learn

Answers: 1. ㄱ - b ㄴ - a   2. door / gate   3. a

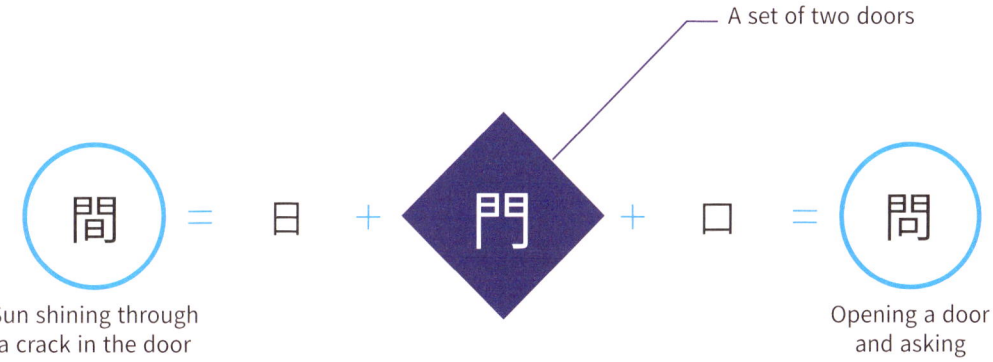

 내 inside

🎵 Track 72

A man goes (入) inside through the entrance (冂).

Character	Pronunciation	Meaning
內	내 [nae]	inside

✂ Breakdown

| 內 | 冂 | symbol | entrance |
| 內 | 入 | 입 | enter |

✏ Stroke Order

Examples

국내 (gung-nae)	國內	country + inside = domestic
내용 (nae-yong)	內容	inside + face/content = content
안내 (an-nae)	案內	desk/thought + inside = guide
시내 (si-nae)	市內	city + inside = downtown

Sample Sentences

그 편지 내용(內容)이 뭐예요? = What's the content of that letter?

아까 안내(案內) 방송이 나왔어요. = There was an announcement earlier.

이따가 시내(市內)에 갈 거예요. = I will go downtown later.

 south

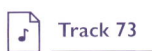 Track 73

A clear-sounding percussion instrument (鬥) with hanging decorations (十) used in southern China, which eventually came to mean south.

Character	Pronunciation	Meaning
南	남 [nam]	south

Breakdown

南	十	symbol	hanging decorations
南	鬥	symbol	musical instrument

Sidenote

Certain tribes in southern China still have a traditional instrument called "南."

Stroke Order

南 南 南 南 南 南 南 南 南

202 Your First Hanja Guide

Examples

강남 gang-nam	江南	river + south = Gangnam, district south of the Han River
남해 na-mae	南海	south + sea = South Sea

Sample Sentences

강남(江南)역에서 만날까? = Shall we meet at Gangnam Station?

여름에 남해(南海)로 휴가 갈 거예요. = I will go on vacation to the South Sea in the summer.

 city / market

 Track 74

Back in the day, shop signs in markets were pieces of fabric (巾) hanging from a horizontal pole with a top frame (亠). A place with many markets is a 'city.'

Character	Pronunciation	Meaning
市	시 [si]	city, market

Breakdown

市	亠	symbol	top frame
市	巾	건	towel

Stroke Order

Examples

시장 si-jang	市場	market + yard = market
도시 do-si	都市	city + city = city
시청 si-cheong	市廳	city + government office = city hall
출시 chul-ssi	出市	be born/go out + market = launch, hit the market
시민 si-min	市民	city + people = citizen

Sample Sentences

시장(市場)에서 채소를 샀어요. = I bought vegetables at the market.

부산은 아주 큰 도시(都市)예요. = Busan is a very big city.

새로운 제품이 어제 출시(出市)됐어요. = A new product was launched yesterday.

 우 rain

Track 75

Combination of raindrops (丶) falling (冂) from the sky (一), meaning rain.

Character	Pronunciation	Meaning
雨	우 [u]	rain

✏️ Stroke Order

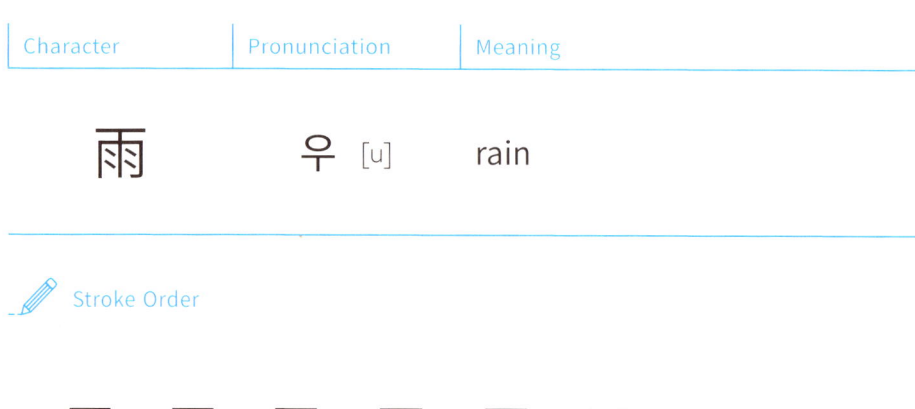

Examples

우산   雨傘   rain + umbrella = umbrella
u-san

우비   雨備   rain + prepare = raincoat
u-bi

Sample Sentences

우산(雨傘)이 없어요.   = I don't have an umbrella.

우비(雨備)를 하나 살까요?   = Shall we buy a raincoat?

Review Quiz

1. Match the character to its sound!

ㄱ. 市   a. 우

ㄴ. 雨   b. 남

ㄷ. 南   c. 시

2. What does this character mean?

雨   =   (   )

3. Find the character that is common among the following words and choose its English meaning.

國內국내   內容내용
案內안내   市內시내

a. market   b. city   c. south   d. inside

Answers: 1. ㄱ - c   ㄴ - a   ㄷ - b   2. rain   3. d

Flow Chart

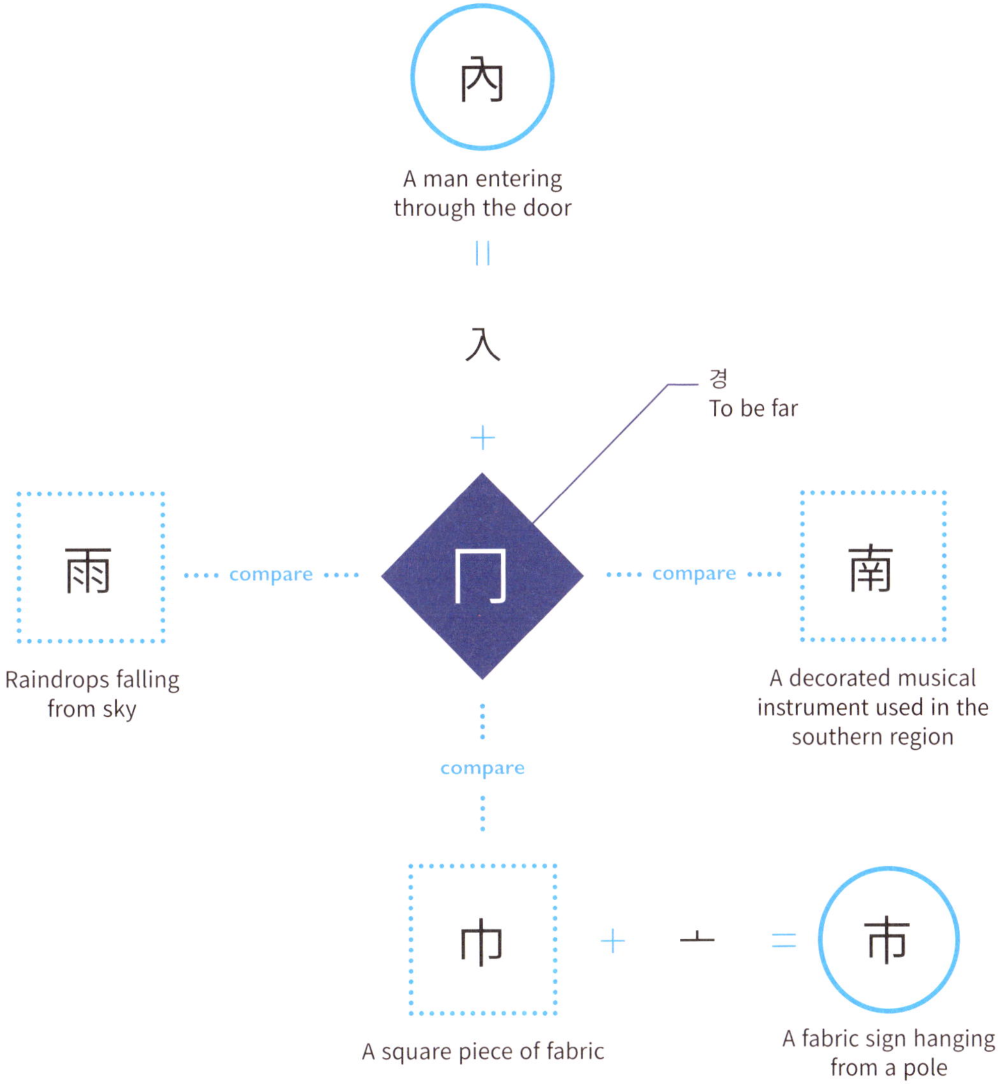

內

A man entering through the door

‖

入

+

경
To be far

雨 ···· compare ···· 冂 ···· compare ···· 南

Raindrops falling from sky

A decorated musical instrument used in the southern region

compare

巾 + 亠 = 市

A square piece of fabric

A fabric sign hanging from a pole

Learn Essential Chinese Characters Used in the Korean Language

Hanja Yut-Nori

1. Prepare some Yut sticks or dice.

2. In case you use dice, 1 is Doh, 2 is Gae, 3 is Gul, 4 is Yut, and 5 is Moh. 6 is "go back one."

3. Start the game at '출발.' Roll the dice or throw the Yut sticks. Move that many spaces by following the blue arrows around the outside of the board.

4. If you land on a corner space, you can take a shortcut through the middle.

5. If you land on a spot with a dotted arrow, you must follow the dotted arrow on your next turn. The two characters connect to form one Korean word.

6. Say the Chinese character of the spot you land on. If you don't remember, go back to where you came from.

7. The first person to return to 출발 wins!

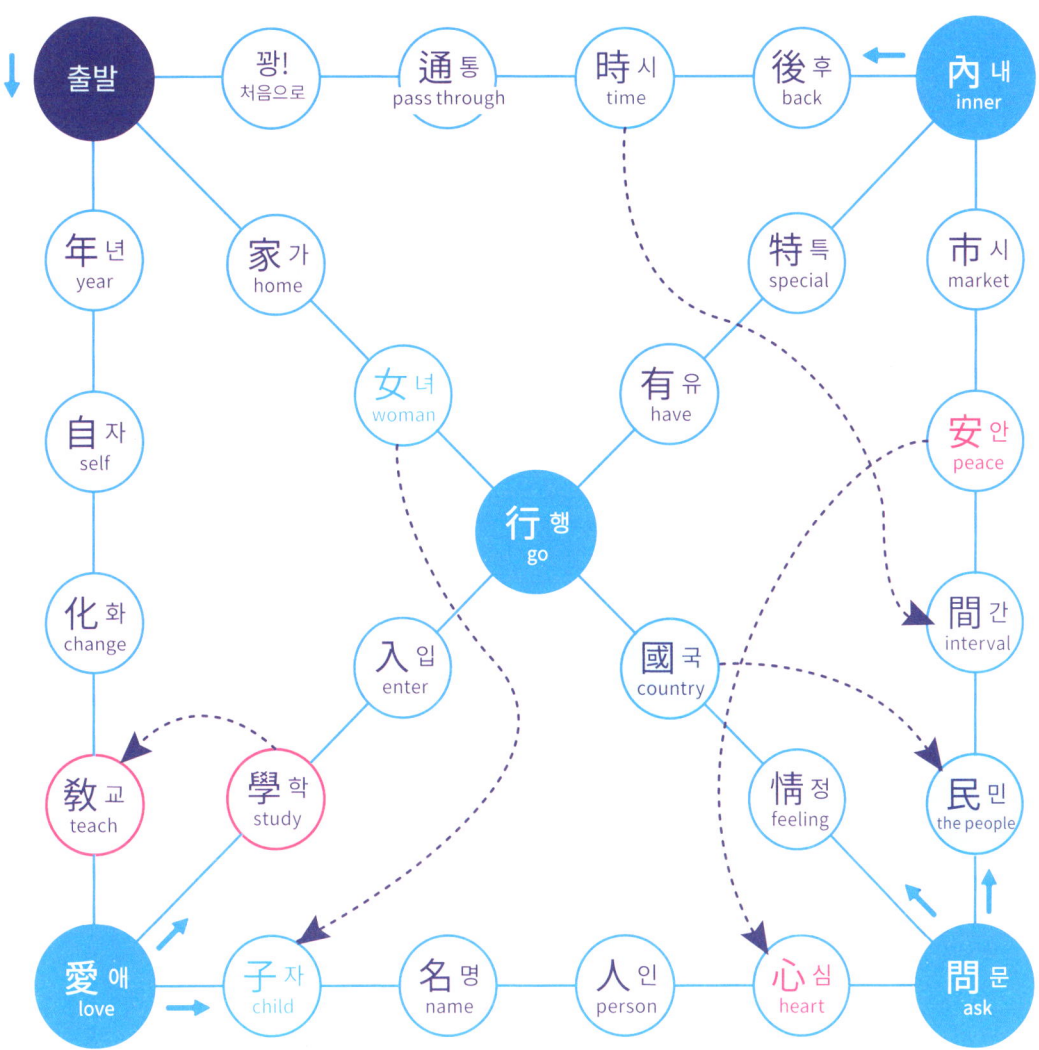

Learn Essential Chinese Characters Used in the Korean Language

Tools

火 — 秋 — 無 — 點 — 力 —

男 — 動 — 食 — 會 — 金 —

 화 fire

 Track 76

A simple pictograph of fire.

Character	Pronunciation	Meaning
火	화 [hwa]	fire

 Stroke Order

火   火   火   火

Examples

화요일 hwa-yo-il	火曜日	fire + day of the week = Tuesday
화재 hwa-jae	火災	fire + disaster = fire, blaze
화산 hwa-san	火山	fire + mountain = volcano
화성 hwa-seong	火星	fire + star = Mars
소화기 so-hwa-gi	消火器	disappear + fire + container = fire extinguisher
화상 hwa-sang	火傷	fire + hurt = burn, scald

Sample Sentences

화요일(火曜日)에 뭐 해요? = What are you going to do on Tuesday?

이 건물에는 소화기(消火器)가 없어요. = This building doesn't have fire extinguishers.

화상(火傷) 입었어요? = Did you get burned?

 추 autumn / fall

 Track 77

Rice (禾) fields that are catching fire (火) is another way of saying the rice is ripe and almost ready to harvest. This also means it is autumn.

Character	Pronunciation	Meaning
秋	추 [chu]	autumn, fall

 Breakdown

| 秋 | 禾 | 화 | rice plant |
| 秋 | 火 | 화 | fire |

Sidenote

Chinese people liken the autumn rice (禾) paddies to a field that caught fire (火).

Stroke Order

秋 秋 秋 秋 秋 秋 秋 秋 秋

Examples

| 추석 chu-seok | 秋夕 | fall + evening = Chuseok, Korean harvest festival |

| 추수 chu-su | 秋收 | fall + harvest = harvest |

Sample Sentences

추석(秋夕)에 친척들을 만나요. = I meet my relatives during Chuseok.

 nothingness

 Track 78

This character represents the shape of a shaman holding a sacred object like a feather, and dancing in a trance so fast that their feet are only visible as four dots (灬). Because the feet are almost invisible, the character also means 'none.'

Character	Pronunciation	Meaning
無	무 [mu]	nothingness, none

✂ Breakdown

無	𠂉	symbol	a shaman dancing
無	灬	symbol	four dots

Sidenote

Even now in China, shamans dance with swords decorated with feathers or tassels.

✏ Stroke Order

218   Your First Hanja Guide

Examples

한글	漢字	뜻
무시 mu-si	無視	nothingness + see = disregard
무조건 mu-jo-kkeon	無條件	none + condition = unconditional
무효 mu-hyo	無效	none + effect = invalidity, invalid
무작정 mu-jak-jjeong	無酌定	none + decision = blindly, thoughtlessly
무료 mu-ryo	無料	none + fee = free of charge
무선 mu-seon	無線	none + line = wireless
허무 heo-mu	虛無	empty + nothingness = futility
무사 mu-sa	無事	nothingness + work = safe
무지 mu-ji	無知	nothingness + know = ignorance
무죄 mu-joe	無罪	none + sin = innocence

Sample Sentences

무시(無視)하지 마세요. = Don't ignore me.

무작정(無酌定) 기차를 탔어요. = I got on a train without any plans.

무료(無料)로 다운 받을 수 있어요. = You can download it for free.

 點 dot / spot

 Track 79

To make a character meaning 'dot', the Chinese used the character for "black 黑" and combined it with "occupy 占" to borrow the pronunciation.

Character	Pronunciation	Meaning
點	점 [jeom]	dot, spot, point, aspect

Breakdown

點	黑	흑	black

Footnote
"黑" - Fire (灬) causes black smoke to rise into the chimney (四) and exit (土), blackening everything around it.

點	占	점	occupy

Stroke Order

點 點 點 點 點 點 點 點 點
點 點 點 點 點 點 點 點

Examples

점수 jeom-su	點數	point + rating =	score, point
장점 jang-jjeom	長點	good + aspect =	advantage
단점 dan-jjeom	短點	short + aspect =	shortcoming
채점 chae-jjeom	採點	distinguish + point =	marking
강점 gang-jjeom	强點	strong + aspect =	strength, strong point
약점 yak-jjeom	弱點	weak + aspect =	weakness
원점 won-jjeom	原點	origin + point =	starting point
점선 jeom-seon	點線	dot + line =	dotted line
동점 dong-jjeom	同點	same + point =	tie

Sample Sentences

시험 점수(點數) 나왔어요? = Did you get your exam scores?

장점(長點)을 찾아봐요. = Try looking for an advantage.

점선(點線)을 따라 선을 그려 봐요. = Try drawing a line along the dotted lines.

Review Quiz

1. Match the character to its sound!

ㄱ. 點　　　　　　　　a. 점

ㄴ. 無　　　　　　　　b. 무

ㄷ. 秋　　　　　　　　c. 추

2. What does this character mean?

無　＝　(　　　　　)

3. Find the character that is common among the following words and choose its English meaning.

> 火災화재　　火山화산
> 消火器소화기　　火傷화상

a. dot　　b. point　　c. autumn/fall　　d. fire

Answers:　1. ㄱ-a ㄴ-b ㄷ-c　2. nothingness　3. d

Flow Chart

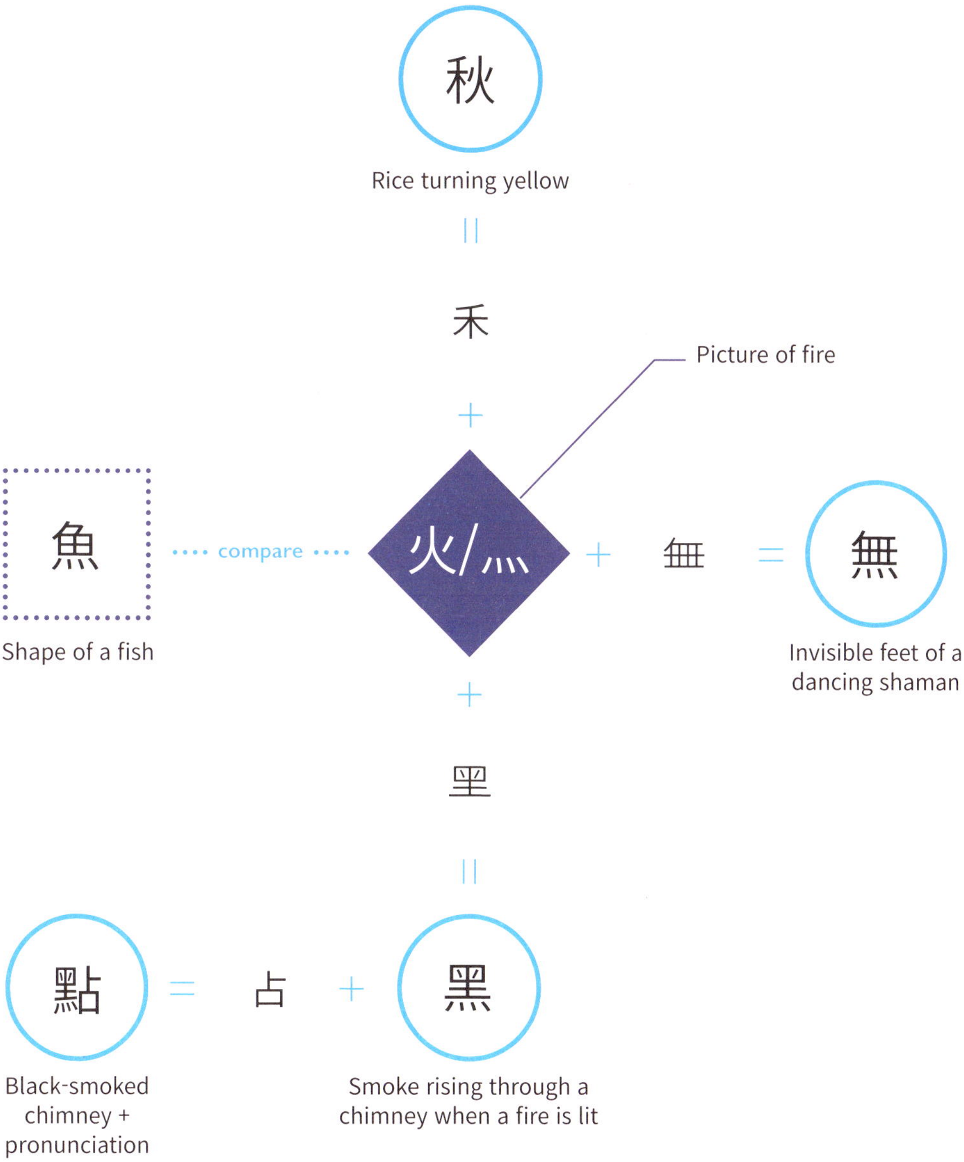

秋
Rice turning yellow

=

禾

+

火/灬 — Picture of fire

魚 ···· compare ···· + 𣍟 = 無
Shape of a fish   Invisible feet of a dancing shaman

+

黑

=

點 = 占 + 黑
Black-smoked chimney + pronunciation   Smoke rising through a chimney when a fire is lit

 력 power

 Track 80

Symbolizes plow, a critical tool in agriculture. Power is needed to pull the plow in the fields.

Character	Pronunciation	Meaning
力	력 [ryeok]	power, strength

 Stroke Order

力　力

Examples

노력 no-ryeok	努力	make an effort + power = effort
능력 neung-nyeok	能力	proficient + power = ability
협력 hyeom-nyeok	協力	harmony/help + power = collaboration
매력 mae-ryeok	魅力	fascinate + power = charm
학력 hang-nyeok	學力	learn + strength = academic ability, academic background
체력 che-ryeok	體力	body + strength = physical strength, stamina
기억력 gi-eong-nyeok	記憶力	record + think + power = memory

Sample Sentences

앞으로 이 팀과 함께 협력(協力)할 거예요. = We will collaborate with this team from now on.

저 여자 정말 매력(魅力)이 넘쳐요. = She's really charming. (lit. She is overflowing with charm.)

저는 기억력(記憶力)이 좋아요. = I have a good memory.

 남 man

Track 81

Signifies a man working in the field (田) using a plow (力).

Character	Pronunciation	Meaning
男	남 [nam]	man

Breakdown

男	田	전	field
男	力	력	power

Stroke Order

男 男 男 男 男 男 男

Examples

남자 nam-ja	男子	man + son/person =	man
남편 nam-pyeon	男便	man + comfortable =	husband
남녀 nam-nyeo	男女	man + woman =	man and woman
남매 nam-mae	男妹	man + sister =	brother and sister
장남 jang-nam	長男	firstborn + man =	the oldest son
미남 mi-nam	美男	beautiful + man =	good-looking man
남학생 na-mak-ssaeng	男學生	man + student =	male student

Sample Sentences

남편(男便)은 같이 안 왔어요.
= My husband didn't come with me.

남매(男妹)가 정말 닮았어요.
= The brother and the sister really look alike.

남학생(男學生)들은 교실에 들어가세요.
= Male students, please go to your classrooms.

 동 move

 Track 82

This character shows the moving of a plow (力) to distribute seeds inside a heavy (重) sack.

Character	Pronunciation	Meaning
動	동 [dong]	move

Breakdown

動	重	중	heavy

Footnote
"重" - Signifies a person (千→人) carrying a heavy sack (里→東) on his back.

動	力	력	power

Stroke Order

動 動 動 動 動 動 動 動
動 動 動

228   Your First Hanja Guide

Examples

한글	漢字	의미
동물 dong-mul	動物	move + thing = animal
동물원 dong-mu-rwon	動物園	animal + hill/yard = zoo
감동 gam-dong	感動	feel + move = touched, touching
부동산 bu-dong-san	不動産	not + move + property = real estate
동기 dong-gi	動機	move + chance = motive
행동 haeng-dong	行動	go + move = act, action
이동 i-dong	移動	shift + move = movement (to a different location)
활동 hwal-ttong	活動	live + move = activity
노동 no-dong	勞動	work + move = labor
충동 chung-dong	衝動	stab/surge + move = impulse
작동 jak-ttong	作動	make + move = (machine) operation, working, running

Sample Sentences

일요일에 동물원(動物園)에 갔어요.   = I went to the zoo on Sunday.

정말 감동(感動) 받았어요.   = I was really touched.

청소기가 작동(作動)을 안 해요.   = My vacuum cleaner doesn't work.

Review Quiz

1. Match the character to its sound!

ㄱ. 動   a. 동

ㄴ. 力   b. 력

2. What does this character mean?

力   =   (   )

3. Find the character that is common among the following words and choose its English meaning.

> 男子남자   男女남녀
> 長男장남   男學生남학생

a. move   b. man   c. woman   d. student

Answers: 1. ㄱ - a   ㄴ - b   2. power   3. b

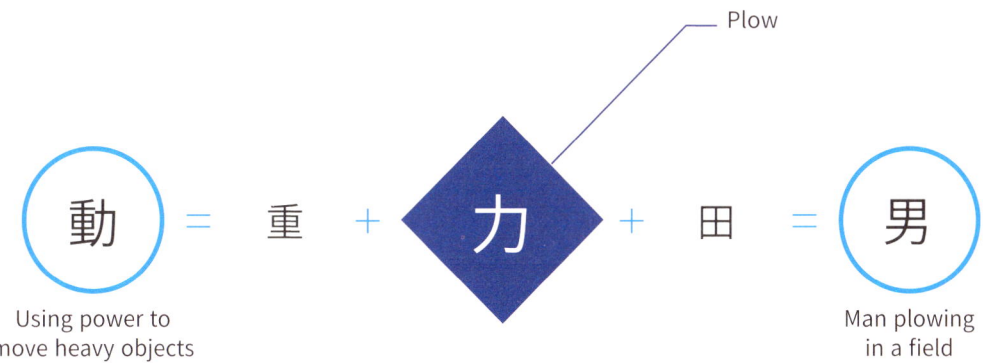

 식 eat / food

 Track 83

A bowl of food (艮) and a lid (亼) to keep it warm means 'food or to eat.'

Character	Pronunciation	Meaning
食	식 [sik]	eat, food, meal

Sidenote

"亼" - A container and its lid must be assembled or kept together.

Stroke Order

Examples

음식 eum-sik	飲食	drink + eat = food
음식점 eum-sik-jjeom	飲食店	drink + eat + store = restaurant
식사 sik-ssa	食事	meal + work = have a meal
식탁 sik-tak	食卓	meal + high = dinner table

Korean	Hanja	Breakdown
식당 sik-ttang	食堂	meal + house = restaurant
간식 gan-sik	間食	gap + meal = snack
식구 sik-kku	食口	meal + mouth = family
외식 oe-sik	外食	outside + eat = eating out
식욕 si-gyok	食慾	eat + greed = appetite
과식 gwa-sik	過食	overflow + eat = overeating
채식 chae-sik	菜食	vegetable + eat = vegetarian diet
회식 hoe-sik	會食	gather + eat = company dinner
분식 bun-sik	粉食	powder + meal = flour-based food
조식 jo-sik	朝食	morning + meal = breakfast

Sample Sentences

식사(食事)했어요? = Have you eaten yet?
(lit. Have you had a meal?)

오늘 밤에 외식(外食)할 거예요. = I am going out to eat tonight.

저는 채식(菜食)주의자예요. = I am a vegetarian.

 회 gather

 Track 84

This image represents gathering (亼) several ingredients to put into the steamer (罒+曰) to either steam or boil.

Character	Pronunciation	Meaning
會	회 [hoe]	gather

✂ Breakdown

會	亼	집	gather
會	曾	symbol	stacked dual-pot steamer

Footnote
"曾" - The shape of a stacked dual-pot steamer consists of a pot (曰) for boiling water on bottom and a steaming tray with holes (罒) on top.

✏ Stroke Order

會 會 會 會 會 會 會 會
會 會 會 會 會

Examples

한글	한자	뜻
기회 gi-hoe	機會	opportunity + gather = opportunity
사회 sa-hoe	社會	gather + gather = society
국회 gu-koe	國會	country + gather = National Assembly
회사 hoe-sa	會社	gather + gather = company
회의 hoe-ui	會議	gather + discuss = conference
회장 hoe-jang	會長	gather + adult/leader = chairman, president
회원 hoe-won	會員	gather + member = member
대회 dae-hoe	大會	big + gather = convention, conference, competition, championship
회계 hoe-gye	會計	gather + count = accounting
면회 myeo-noe	面會	face + gather = visit (someone at a hospital/prison/army)

Sample Sentences

기회(機會)를 한 번만 더 주세요. = Please give me just one more opportunity.

오늘 회사(會社) 쉬는 날이에요. = Today is a day off for our company.

중요한 회의(會議)가 두 개 있어요. = I have two important meetings.

  metal / gold

 Track 85

Metals (丶) taken from the earth (土) were melted and poured into a cast (仝). This character came to represent gold because it was one of the first valuable metals to attract human attention – it is beautiful, easy to manipulate, and does not rust.

Character	Pronunciation	Meaning
金	금 [geum]	metal, gold, money

Sidenote

Gold is actually the earliest of metals to be used by humans, it first being used in Mesopotamia around 3,000 B.C.

Stroke Order

Examples

금요일 geu-myo-il	金曜日	gold + day of the week = Friday
세금 se-geum	稅金	tax + money = tax
벌금 beol-geum	罰金	punish + money = fine, penalty
장학금 jang-hak-kkeum	奬學金	encourage + learn + money = scholarship
현금 hyeon-geum	現金	cash + money = cash
저금 jeo-geum	貯金	pile + money = saving
송금 song-geum	送金	send + money = wire, transfer
요금 yo-geum	料金	price + money = charge, fee

Sample Sentences

늦으면 벌금(罰金)을 내야 해요. = You have to pay a fine if you are late.

올해도 장학금(奬學金)을 받았어요. = I got a scholarship again this year.

지금 현금(現金) 있어요? = Do you have cash on you now?

Review Quiz

1. Match the character to its sound!

ㄱ. 金   a. 금

ㄴ. 會   b. 회

2. What does this character mean?

金 = (   )

3. Find the character that is common among the following words and choose its English meaning.

> 飮食음식   食卓식탁
> 菜食채식   外食외식

a. eat/food   b. table   c. house   d. vegetable

Answers: 1. ㄱ - a ㄴ - b   2. metal / gold   3. a

Flow Chart

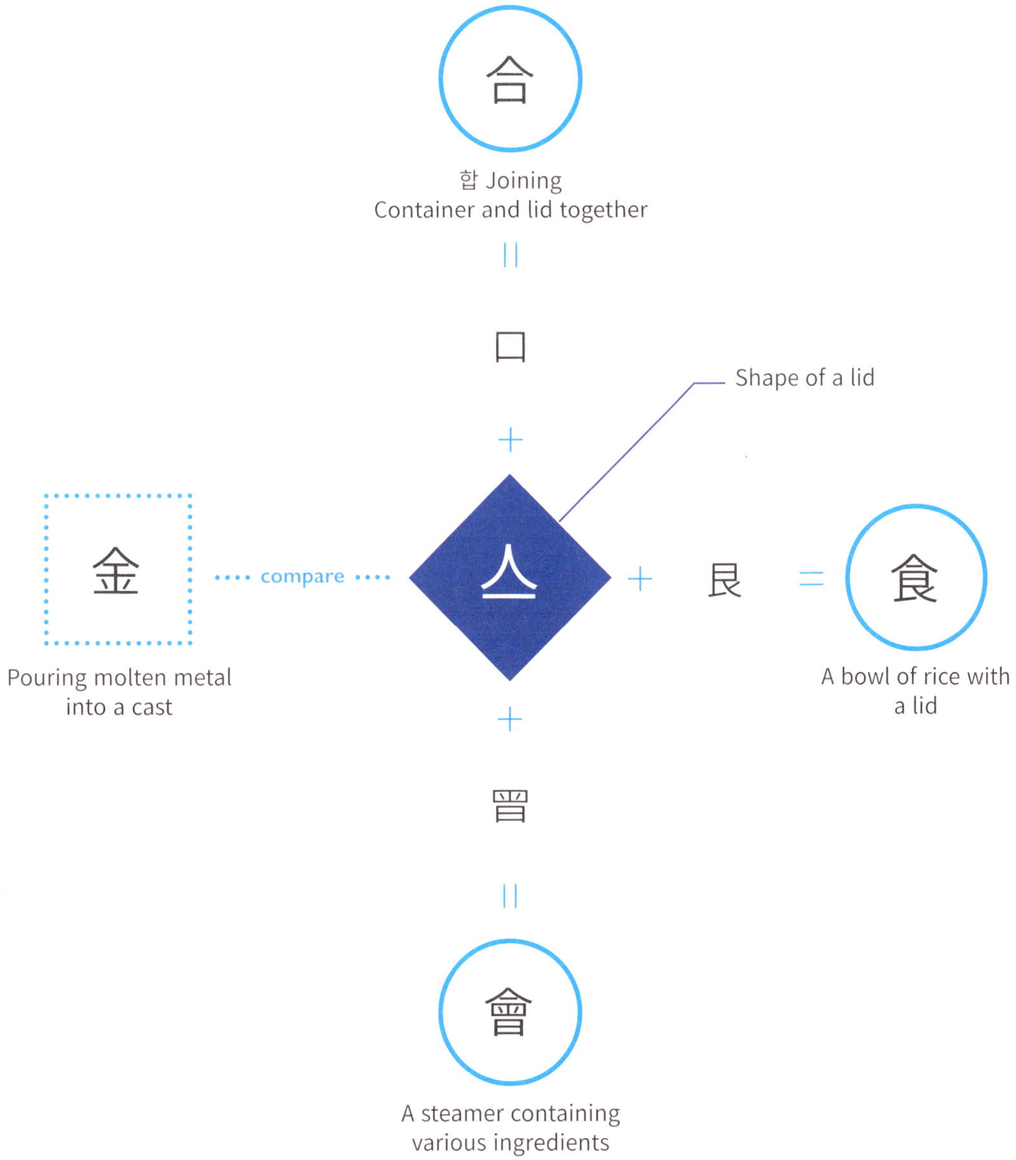

合
합 Joining
Container and lid together

=

口

+

亼 — Shape of a lid

金 ···· compare ···· 亼 + 艮 = 食

Pouring molten metal
into a cast

A bowl of rice with
a lid

+

曰

=

會

A steamer containing
various ingredients

Animals

牛 — 半 — 分 — 公 — 眞 —

 **COW**

 Track 86

Symbolizes a cow with horns when looked at from the front.

Character	Pronunciation	Meaning
牛	우 [u]	cow

✏️ **Stroke Order**

Examples

우유 牛乳   cow + milk = milk
u-yu

Sample Sentences

우유(牛乳) 많이 마시면 키 커요? = Do people grow tall if they drink a lot of milk?

 반 half

 Track 87

Represents a cow (牛) which is being butchered and cut in half (八). A cow signifies good possibilities.

Character	Pronunciation	Meaning
半	반 [ban]	half

✂ Breakdown

半	八	팔	divide/eight

Footnote
"八" is a symbol of symmetry in half, signifying to divide.

半	牛	우	cow

✏ Stroke Order

244　　　Your First Hanja Guide

Examples

한글	한자	의미
절반 jeol-ban	折半	cut + half = half
상반기 sang-ban-gi	上半期	top + half + period = the first half of the year
하반기 ha-ban-gi	下半期	bottom + half + period = the second half of the year
반세기 ban-se-gi	半世紀	half + 100 years + time = half a century
전반 jeon-ban	前半	front + half = the first half
후반 hu-ban	後半	back + half = the second half
반지 ban-ji	半指	half + finger = ring
반숙 ban-suk	半熟	half + ripen/cook = soft-boiled

Sample Sentences

전반(前半)전은 저희가 이겼어요.   = We won the first half of the game.

이건 결혼 반지(半指)예요.   = This is my wedding ring.

계란은 반숙(半熟)으로 해 주세요.   = Please soft-boil my egg.

 분 **divide / minute**

 Track 88

To divide in half (八) with a knife (刀). A 'minute' is a division of time.

Character	Pronunciation	Meaning
分	분 [bun]	divide, minute, share

Breakdown

分	八	팔	divide/eight
分	刀	도	knife

Stroke Order

分 分 分 分

Examples

충분 chung-bun	充分	fill/full + share = enough
부분 bu-bun	部分	group + divide = part
분석 bun-seok	分析	divide + split = analysis
대부분 dae-bu-bun	大部分	big + group + divide = most
분명 bun-myeong	分明	divide + bright = clear
분야 bu-nya	分野	divide + field = area, field
수분 su-bun	水分	water + divide = moisture
성분 seong-bun	成分	form/consist of + divide = ingredient
당분간 dang-bun-gan	當分間	proper + divide + while = for a while

Sample Sentences

이걸로 충분(充分)해요.   = This is enough.

대부분(大部分) 참석할 거예요.   = Most people will participate.

당분간(當分間) 사무실에 없을 거예요.   = I will be out of the office for a while.

 公 public

 Track 89

The womb opens (八) and a fetus (厶) is born. It means that a baby is now a member of the public and no longer under the sole protection of its mother.

Character	Pronunciation	Meaning
公	공 [gong]	public

✂ **Breakdown**

公	八	팔	divide/eight
公	厶	사	newborn baby/private

✎ **Stroke Order**

248　　　Your First Hanja Guide

Examples

공원 gong-won	公園	public + hill/yard = park
공연 gong-yeon	公演	public + spread/act/play = performance, show
공휴일 gong-hyu-il	公休日	public + rest + day = holiday
주인공 ju-in-gong	主人公	owner + person + public = hero, heroine
공개 gong-gae	公開	public + open = make public
공무원 gong-mu-won	公務員	public + work + person = civil servant
공공 gong-gong	公共	public + together = public
공식 gong-sik	公式	public + law/system = formula, formal
공약 gong-yak	公約	public + conclude/promise = pledge

Sample Sentences

친구와 함께 공원(公園)에 갔어요. = I went to the park with my friend.

오늘은 공휴일(公休日)이에요. = Today is a public holiday.

제 아들은 공무원(公務員)이에요. = My son is a civil servant.

 眞 진 truth

 Track 90

Humans place their flawless (直) offerings (匕) on an altar (丌) to the gods to receive their blessing and learn what is true.

Character	Pronunciation	Meaning
眞	진 [jin]	truth

✂ Breakdown

眞	匕	비	spoon
眞	直	직	straight
眞	丌	기	pedestal

Sidenote

Ancient Chinese texts depict the gods using cutlery (匕) to eat the food that was offered in a bronze pot or a cooker with legs (鼎), and then sharing their wisdom and truth with the humans in return.

 Stroke Order

Examples

사진 sa-jin	寫眞	copy + truth =	picture
진지 jin-ji	眞摯	truth + hold =	serious
진실 jin-sil	眞實	truth + truly =	truth
진심 jin-sim	眞心	truth + mind/heart =	sincere, sincerity
순진 sun-jin	純眞	pure + truth =	naive
진품 jin-pum	眞品	truth + product =	genuine article, authentic object

Sample Sentences

사진(寫眞) 찍어 주세요.   = Please take a picture for me.

저 정말 진지(眞摯)해요.   = I am really serious.

너무 순진(純眞)해서 걱정이에요.   = I'm worried because he's so innocent.

Review Quiz

1. Match the character to its sound!

ㄱ. 眞		a. 공	
ㄴ. 公		b. 진	
ㄷ. 分		c. 우	
ㄹ. 牛		d. 분	

2. What does this character mean?

牛　=　(　　　　　)

3. Find the character that is common among the following words and choose its English meaning.

> 折半절반　　前半전반
> 後半후반　　半熟반숙

a. truth　　b. public　　c. half　　d. divide/minute

Answers:　1. ㄱ-b ㄴ-a ㄷ-d ㄹ-c　2. cow　3. c

Flow Chart

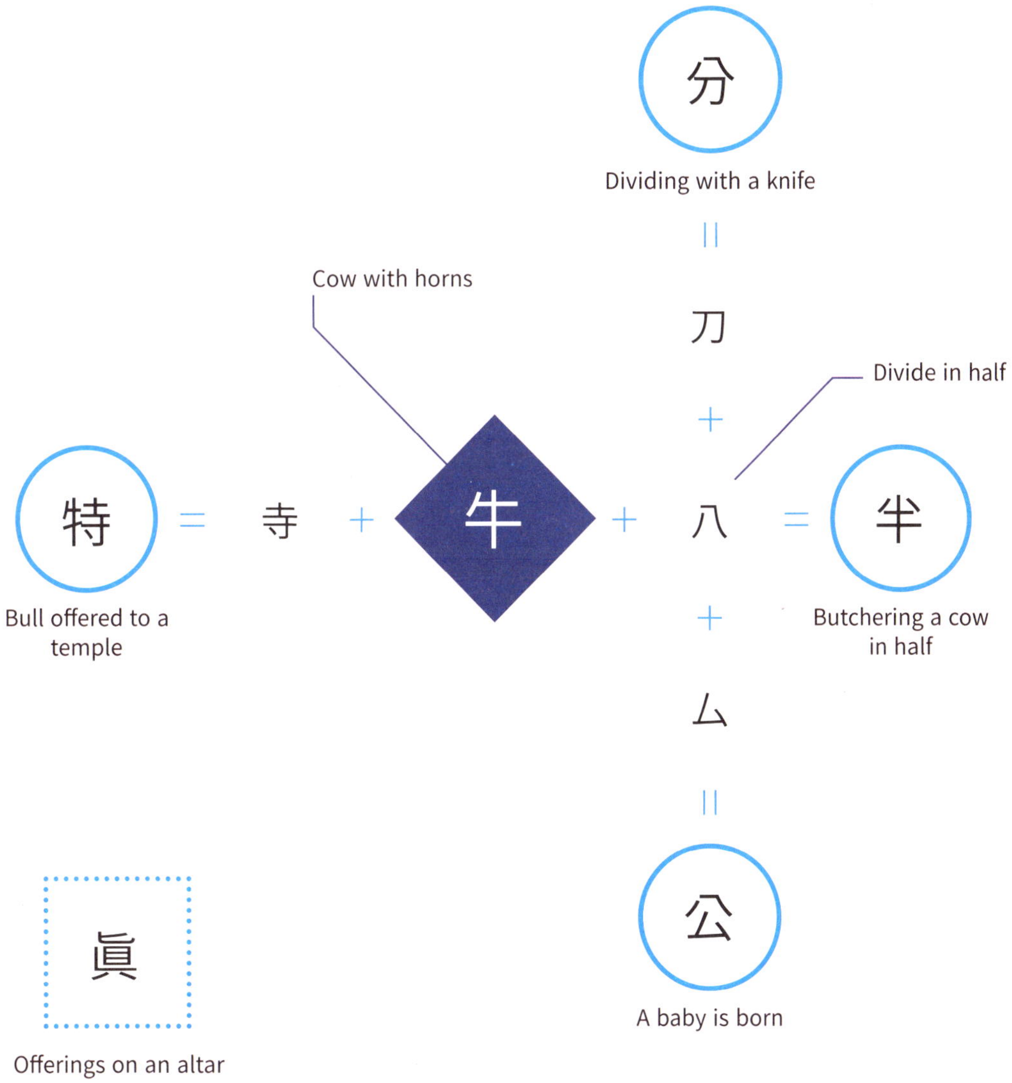

分
Dividing with a knife
=
刀
+
　　　　　　　　　　Divide in half

特 = 寺 + 牛 + 八 = 半

Bull offered to a temple　　　Cow with horns　　　Butchering a cow in half

+
ム
=
公
A baby is born

眞
Offerings on an altar

Learn Essential Chinese Characters Used in the Korean Language

Natural Scenery

木一東一西一重一車一校一來一

樂一味一山一世一茶一生一

 목 tree

🎵 Track 91

Symbolizes a tree by combining branches (一), roots (), and the trunk (|).

Character	Pronunciation	Meaning
木	목 [mok]	tree

✏️ **Stroke Order**

木　木　木　木

Examples

목요일 mo-gyo-il	木曜日	tree + day of the week = Thursday
식목일 sing-mo-gil	植木日	plant + tree + day = Arbor Day
목마 mong-ma	木馬	tree + horse = wooden horse
목재 mok-jjae	木材	tree + ingredient/material = lumber

Sample Sentences

다음 주 목요일(木曜日)에 만나요.   = Let's meet next Thursday.

내일은 식목일(植木日)이에요.   = Tomorrow is Arbor Day.

아빠가 목마(木馬)를 만들어 줬어요.   = My father made a wooden horse for me.

 east

Track 92

The morning sun (日) rising from the east and catching on a tree (木) means 'east'.

Character	Pronunciation	Meaning
東	동 [dong]	east

✂ **Breakdown**

| 東 | 木 | 목 | tree |
| 東 | 日 | 일 | sun |

Sidenote

East, an abstract concept of direction, was something difficult to represent by symbols, and so this character was taken due to its identical pronunciation. Used together with "west 西", which was a very common type of pottery that could be seen anywhere, it meant 'things' in general.

✏ **Stroke Order**

Examples

동해
dong-hae

東海

east + sea = the East Sea

동양
dong-yang

東洋

east + ocean = the Orient, the East

Sample Sentences

주말에 동해(東海) 갈까요?

= Shall we go to the East Sea over the weekend?

 서 west

 Track 93

Symbolizes an earthenware (凵) jar that holds water, with a lid (襾) on top. Borrowed to mean the concept of west since the pronunciation is same.

Character	Pronunciation	Meaning
西	서 [seo]	west

Breakdown

西	襾	아	cover
西	凵	symbol	pottery

Stroke Order

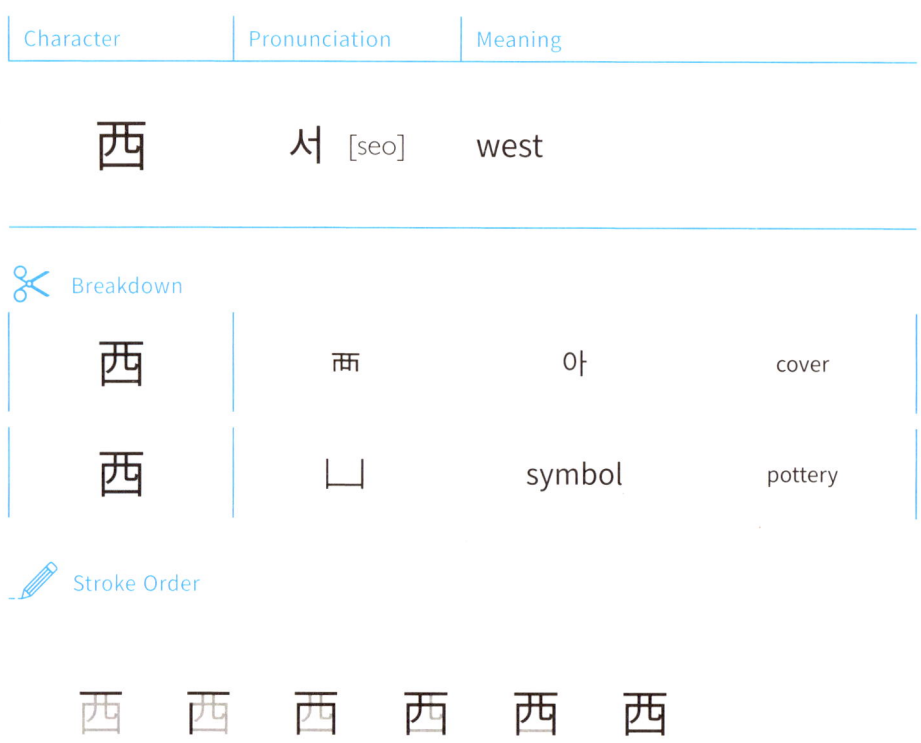

Examples

서해 seo-hae　　西海　　　　west + sea = the West Sea, the Yellow Sea

서양 seo-yang　　西洋　　　west + ocean = the West

Sample Sentences

서해(西海)에서 일몰을 봤어요.　　= I saw the sun set over the West Sea.

 heavy

 Track 94

Represents a person (人) carrying a heavy sack (東) on his back.

Character	Pronunciation	Meaning
重	중 [jung]	heavy, careful, precious

Breakdown

重	千→人	인	person
重	里→東	동	sack/east

Stroke Order

重 重 重 重 重 重 重 重 重

Examples

중요 jung-yo	重要	heavy + important = important
신중 sin-jung	愼重	refrain + careful = caution
존중 jon-jung	尊重	high + precious = respect
중복 jung-bok	重複	heavy + overlap = repetition
소중 so-jung	所重	way/place + precious = precious
체중 che-jung	體重	body + heavy = bodyweight
정중 jeong-jung	鄭重	country name + heavy = polite
귀중 gwi-jung	貴重	precious + precious = precious

Sample Sentences

신중(愼重)하게 결정하세요. = Decide carefully.

제 뜻을 존중(尊重)해 주세요. = Please respect my decision.

중복(重複)해서 사용할 수 없어요. = You cannot use the same thing multiple times.

Learn Essential Chinese Characters Used in the Korean Language

 cart / car

🎵 Track 95

The shape of a cart with wheels, drawn by a horse or an ox. Now it means 'car.'

Character	Pronunciation	Meaning
車	차 [cha, geo]	cart, car

✏️ Stroke Order

車 車 車 車 車 車 車

Examples

자동차 ja-dong-cha	自動車	oneself + move + cart = car
주차장 ju-cha-jang	駐車場	stay + car + yard = parking lot
기차 gi-cha	汽車	steam + car = train
차선 cha-seon	車線	car + line = traffic lane

구급차 gu-geup-cha	救急車	rescue + urgent + car =	ambulance
세차 se-cha	洗車	wash + car =	car wash
마차 ma-cha	馬車	horse + cart =	carriage
유모차 yu-mo-cha	乳母車	milk + mother + cart =	stroller
자전거 ja-jeon-geo	自轉車	oneself + roll + cart =	bicycle
정거장 jeong-geo-jang	停車場	stay + car + yard =	station

Sample Sentences

주차장(駐車場)에 자동차(自動車)를 주차했어요. = I parked my car in the parking lot.

내일 기차(汽車) 타고 여행 가요. = I am going on a trip tomorrow by train.

아침에 세차(洗車)했어요. = I washed my car this morning.

Review Quiz

1. Match the character to its sound!

ㄱ. 重   a. 서

ㄴ. 西   b. 목

ㄷ. 東   c. 중

ㄹ. 木   d. 동

2. What does this character mean?

木 = (　　　　)

3. Find the character that is common among the following words and choose its English meaning.

救急車 구급차　　乳母車 유모차

駐車場 주차장　　汽車 기차

a. heavy   b. cart/car   c. west   d. east

Answers: 1. ㄱ-c ㄴ-a ㄷ-d ㄹ-b   2. tree   3. b

Flow Chart

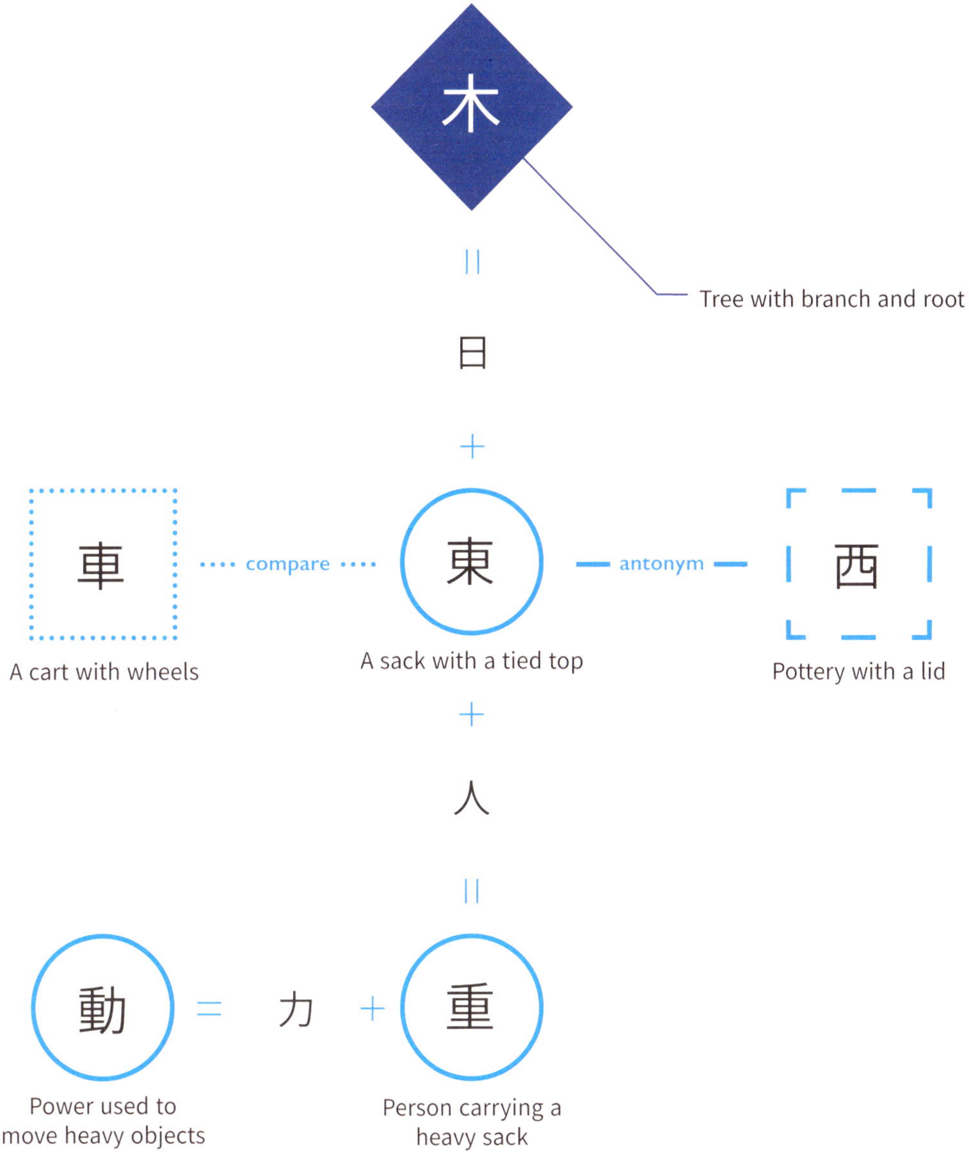

木 — Tree with branch and root

‖

日

+

車 ····compare···· 東 —antonym— 西

A cart with wheels　　A sack with a tied top　　Pottery with a lid

+

人

‖

動 = 力 + 重

Power used to move heavy objects　　Person carrying a heavy sack

Learn Essential Chinese Characters Used in the Korean Language

 school

 Track 96

A school is a structure made of wood (木) where teachers and students get together to exchange (交) knowledge.

Character	Pronunciation	Meaning
校	교 [gyo]	school

✂ Breakdown

校	木	목	tree
校	交	교	associate with

Footnote
"交" - When you see an image of two people (亠) with legs crossed/mixed (父), this character means 'associate with.' For a man and a woman to be in this posture, it also indicates that they are in love with each other and reciprocate each other's feelings.

✏ Stroke Order

Examples

학교 hak-kkyo	學校	learn + school = school
등교 deung-gyo	登校	climb + school = going to school
교장 gyo-jang	校長	school + leader = principal, headmaster
모교 mo-gyo	母校	mother + school = alma mater
교복 gyo-bok	校服	school + clothes = school uniform

Sample Sentences

교장(校長) 선생님이 불러요. = The school principal is calling you.

여기가 제 모교(母校)예요. = This is my alma mater.

교복(校服)이 조금 작아요. = My school uniform is a little small (for me).

 래 / 내 come

 Track 97

Symbolizes barley, which is a crop (木) similar to rice (米). Barley bears its grain in spring after a long winter, so when it sprouts, it signifies that spring is coming.

Character	Pronunciation	Meaning
來	래(내)[lae(nae)]	come

Breakdown

來	木	목	tree
來	米	미	rice

Sidenote

The radical of this letter is a "person 人" but the etymology is not related to "person 人".

Stroke Order

Examples

내일 nae-il	來日	come + day = tomorrow
내년 nae-nyeon	來年	come + year = next year
미래 mi-rae	未來	not + come = future
장래 jang-rae	將來	in the future + come = future
거래 geo-rae	去來	go + come = deal, transaction
원래 wol-rae	元來	first + come = original, originally
유래 yu-rae	由來	come from + come = origin

Sample Sentences

내일(來日) 다시 오세요. = Come again tomorrow.

내년(來年)에 학교에 들어가요. = I am starting school next year.

원래(元來) 자리가 어디예요? = Where is your original seat?

 악 / 락 music / pleasure

 Track 98

Music is symbolized by a drum (白) with a string (絲) decoration standing on a drumstand (木). Also represents joy or pleasure from playing with the decorated drum.

Character	Pronunciation	Meaning
樂	악, 락(낙) [ak, lak(nak)]	music, pleasure, song, enjoy

✂ Breakdown

樂	糸	사	thread/rope
樂	白	백	white
樂	木	목	tree

✏ Stroke Order

Examples

음악 eu-mak	音樂	sound + music = music
오락 o-rak	娛樂	enjoy + pleasure = entertainment, game
오락실 o-rak-ssil	娛樂室	enjoy + pleasure + house/room = (video) arcade
악기 ak-kki	樂器	music + instrument = musical instrument
악보 ak-ppo	樂譜	music + score = music score, sheet music
낙천적 nak-cheon-jeok	樂天的	enjoy + fate + have a character of = optimistic

Sample Sentences

어떤 음악(音樂) 좋아해요? = What kind of music do you like?

아까 오락실(娛樂室)에 있었어요. = I was at the arcade earlier.

그 사람은 정말 낙천적(樂天的)이에요. = He is really optimistic.

 taste

Track 99

A sapling (朱) that is still growing is thin and fragile. This character means to use one's tongue (口) to distinguish very thin and fragile (朱) differences in taste.

Character	Pronunciation	Meaning
味	미 [mi]	taste

Breakdown

| 味 | 口 | 구 | mouth |
| 味 | 未 | 미 | not |

Footnote
"未" - A shorter horizontal line (一) is added to the top of "木" to emphasize that the growth is not yet finished. The tree is, therefore, not great in size, but rather small and still growing.

Stroke Order

味 味 味 味 味 味 味 味

Examples

| 취미
chwi-mi | 趣味 | intention/go toward + taste = hobby |

| 의미
ui-mi | 意味 | meaning + taste = meaning |

| 무의미
mu-ui-mi | 無意味 | none + meaning = meaningless |

| 조미료
jo-mi-ryo | 調味料 | adjust + taste + ingredient = seasoning |

| 미각
mi-gak | 味覺 | taste + realize = palate, taste |

Sample Sentences

취미(趣味)가 뭐예요?   = What is your hobby?

조미료(調味料)가 많이 들어갔어요.   = (The food) has a lot of seasoning.

두 단어는 같은 의미(意味)예요.   = The two words have the same meaning.

Review Quiz

1. Match the character to its sound!

ㄱ. 味　　　　　　　a. 교

ㄴ. 來　　　　　　　b. 래

ㄷ. 校　　　　　　　c. 미

2. What does this character mean?

校　＝　(　　　　　)

3. Find the character that is common among the following words and choose its English meaning.

> 音樂음악　　娛樂오락
> 樂譜악보　　樂器악기

a. music/pleasure　　b. hobby　　c. taste　　d. come

Answers: 1. ㄱ - c ㄴ - b ㄷ - a　2. school　3. a

Flow Chart

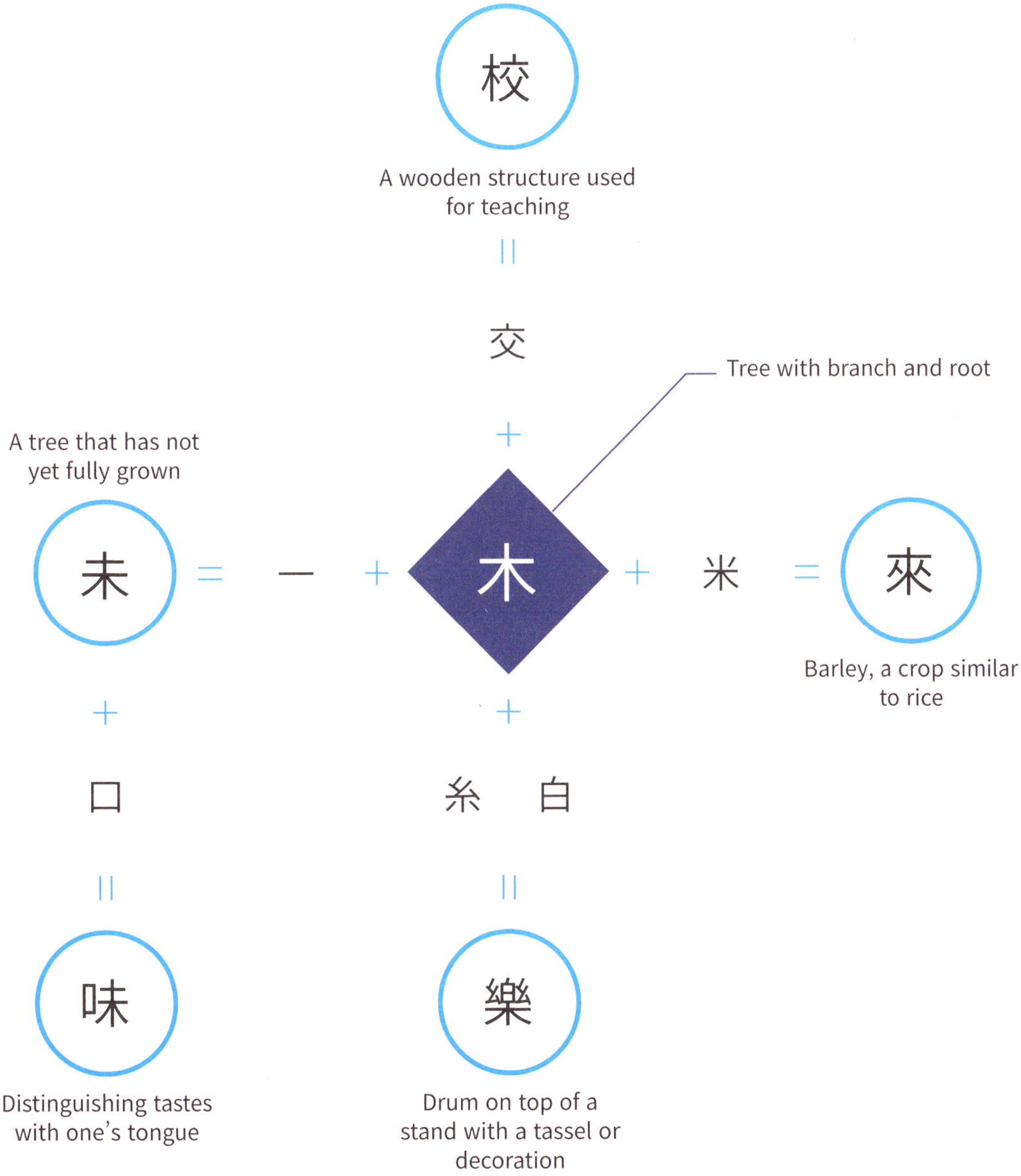

校
A wooden structure used for teaching
=
交
+

未 — A tree that has not yet fully grown

未 = 一 + 木 + 米 = 來

木 — Tree with branch and root

來 — Barley, a crop similar to rice

+   +
口   糸 白
=   =
味   樂

味 — Distinguishing tastes with one's tongue

樂 — Drum on top of a stand with a tassel or decoration

Learn Essential Chinese Characters Used in the Korean Language

 산 mountain

🎵 Track 100

Represents a mountain with a summit and ridges of different heights.

Character	Pronunciation	Meaning
山	산 [san]	mountain

✏️ **Stroke Order**

Examples

등산
deung-san

登山

climb + mountain = hiking

화산
hwa-san

火山

fire + mountain = volcano

Sample Sentences

등산(登山) 좋아해요?   = Do you like hiking?

등산(登山)화를 하나 샀어요.   = I bought a pair of hiking shoes.

화산(火山)이 폭발했어요.   = The volcano erupted.

Represents budding sprouts (屮) on a branch in spring, signifying the beginning of life in a new world.

Character	Pronunciation	Meaning
世	세 [se]	world, lifetime, human

✏️ Stroke Order

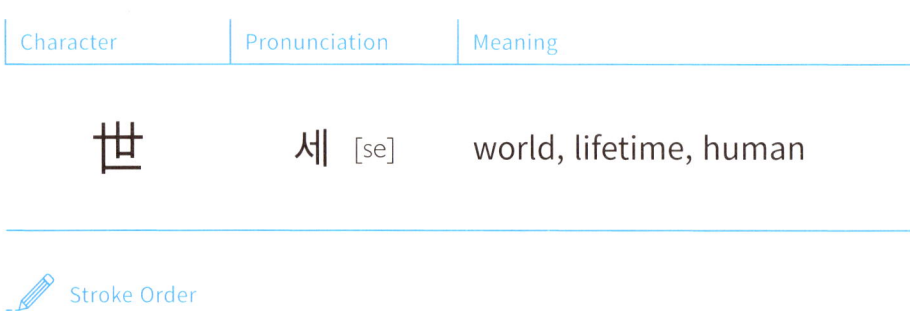

Examples

세계 se-gye	世界	world + border = world
세계 지도 se-gye ji-do	世界 地圖	world + ground + drawing = world map
세계사 se-gye-sa	世界史	world + historical records = world history
세상 se-sang	世上	world + top = world, society
세대 se-dae	世代	human + time/era = generation
차세대 cha-se-dae	次世代	next + generation = next generation
출세 chul-sse	出世	go out + world = success

Sample Sentences

세계 지도(世界 地圖) 있어요? = Do you have a world map?

다음 수업은 세계사(世界史)예요. = The next class is world history.

저 사람 정말 출세(出世)했어요. = That person became really successful.

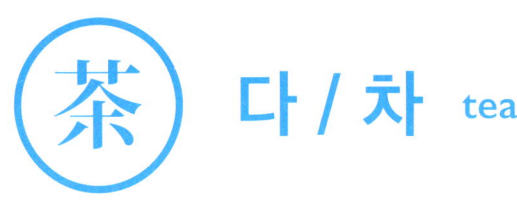 tea

♪ Track 102

Symbolizes the making of tea by processing leaves (艹) that cover (人) the tea plants (木).

Character	Pronunciation	Meaning
茶	다, 차 [da, cha]	tea

 Breakdown

茶	艹	초	grass
茶	人	symbol	covering
茶	木	목	tree

Sidenote

Tea originated from the Szechuan (四川) region of China, and spread to other regions.

✏️ Stroke Order

茶 茶 茶 茶 茶 茶 茶 茶 茶 茶

Examples

다과
da-gwa

茶菓

tea + cookie = refreshments

녹차
nok-cha

綠茶

green color + tea = green tea

홍차
hong-cha

紅茶

red color + tea = black tea

Sample Sentences

뒤에 간단한 다과(茶菓)가 있어요.

= Behind you, there are some simple refreshments.

따뜻한 녹차(綠茶)를 마셨어요.

= I drank hot green tea.

커피 말고 홍차(紅茶) 주세요.

= Please give me black tea instead of coffee.

 be born / life

New sprouts (出) start growing above ground (土), representing birth and life.

Character	Pronunciation	Meaning
生	생 [saeng]	be born, life, live, person, fresh

 Stroke Order

生　生　生　生　生

Examples

생일 saeng-il	生日	be born + day = birthday
선생 seon-saeng	先生	first/earlier + live = teacher
학생 hak-ssaeng	學生	learn + person = student
동생 dong-saeng	同生	together + live = younger brother or sister
평생 pyeong-saeng	平生	flat + live = lifetime
생선 saeng-seon	生鮮	fresh + fish = fish
생수 saeng-su	生水	fresh + water = mineral water
야생 ya-saeng	野生	field + live = wild
생명 saeng-myeong	生命	live + life = life
생산 saeng-san	生産	person + produce = production

Sample Sentences

생일(生日) 축하해요.   = Happy birthday.

저는 여동생(同生)이 한 명 있어요.   = I have a younger sister.

생수(生水) 한 병 주세요.   = Please give me a bottle of mineral water.

Review Quiz

1. Match the character to its sound!

ㄱ. 山   a. 생

ㄴ. 茶   b. 산

ㄷ. 生   c. 다

2. What does this character mean?

茶 = (　　　　)

3. Find the character that is common among the following words and choose its English meaning.

世界세계　　世上세상
世代세대　　出世출세

a. green   b. refreshments   c. mountain   d. world/lifetime

Answers: 1. ㄱ - b　ㄴ - c　ㄷ - a　　2. tea　　3. d

Flow Chart

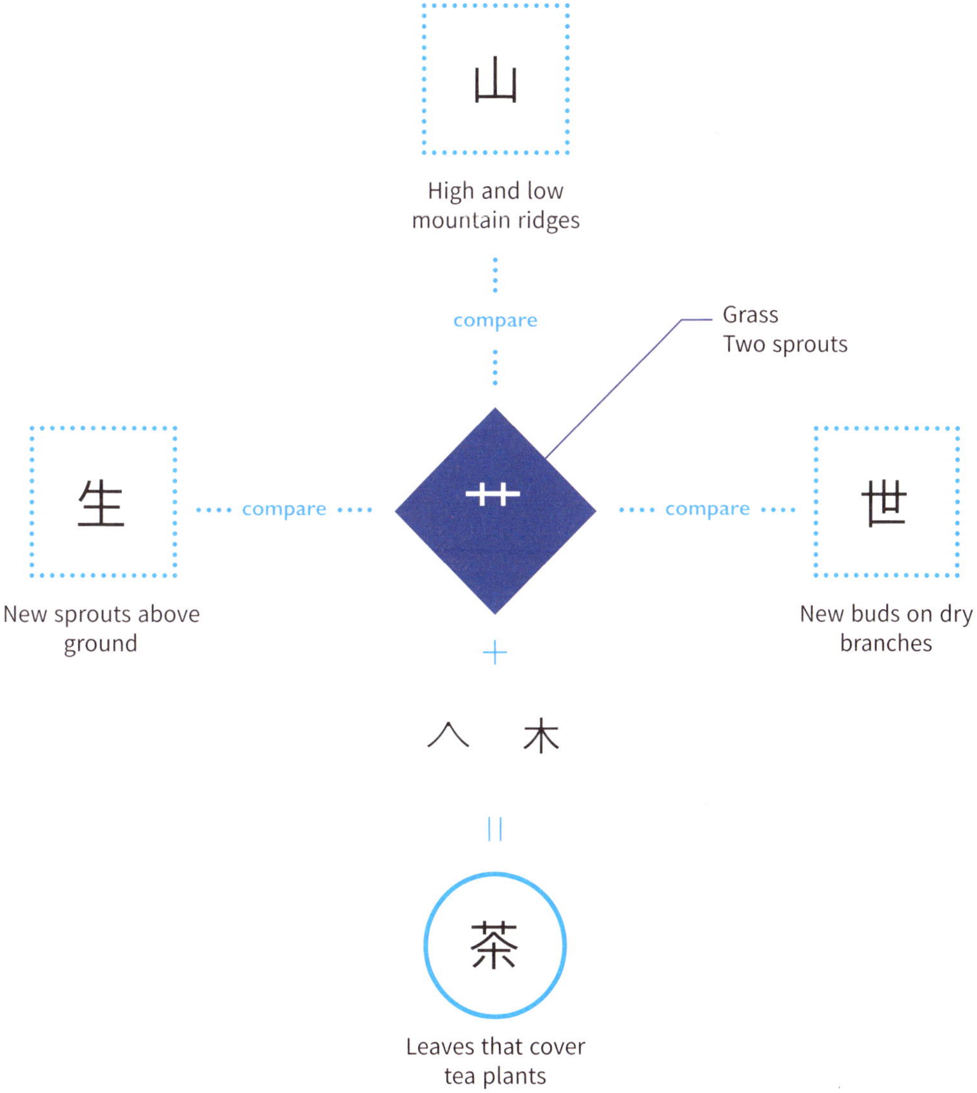

山
High and low mountain ridges

⋯ compare ⋯

Grass
Two sprouts

生 ⋯ compare ⋯ 艹 ⋯ compare ⋯ 世

New sprouts above ground

New buds on dry branches

\+

人　木

＝

茶

Leaves that cover tea plants

Heavenly Bodies

日 — 春 — 月 — 明 — 多 —
前 — 土 — 地 — 場 —

 일 day / sun

 Track 104

Symbolizes the round sun. Also signifies day, a cycle of the sun.

Character	Pronunciation	Meaning
日	일 [il]	day, sun

Stroke Order

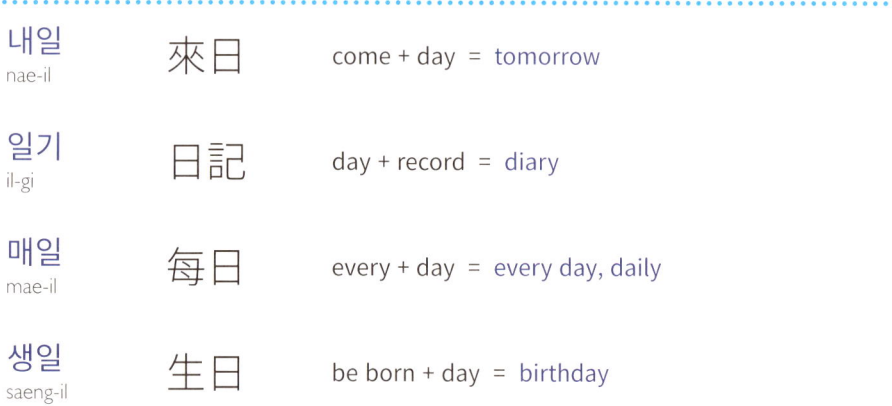

Examples

내일 nae-il	來日	come + day = tomorrow
일기 il-gi	日記	day + record = diary
매일 mae-il	每日	every + day = every day, daily
생일 saeng-il	生日	be born + day = birthday

휴일 hyu-il	休日	rest + day = day off, holiday
공휴일 gong-hyu-il	公休日	public + rest + day = public holiday
일상 il-ssang	日常	day + always = everyday life
당일 dang-il	當日	this/that + day = the very day
일주일 il-jju-il	一週日	one + a week + day = a week, one week
일몰 il-mol	日沒	sun + sink/hide = sunset
일출 il-chul	日出	sun + be born/go out = sunrise

Sample Sentences

내일(來日)은 공휴일(公休日)이에요.　= Tomorrow is a public holiday.

저는 일기(日記)를 매일(每日) 써요.　= I write in my diary every day.

일주일(一週日) 후가 제 생일(生日)이에요.　= My birthday is a week from now.

 spring

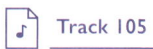 Track 105

As the days grow longer and the sun (日) becomes stronger during the spring, sprouts (夫) begin to emerge.

Character	Pronunciation	Meaning
春	춘 [chun]	spring

✂ Breakdown

春	夫	symbol	sprouts

Footnote
Ancient Chinese texts show "夫" as a group of sprouts (屮).

春	日	일	sun

✏ Stroke Order

春 春 春 春 春 春 春 春 春

Your First Hanja Guide

Examples

사춘기
sa-chun-gi

思春期   think + spring + period = adolescence, puberty

청춘
cheong-chun

靑春   blue/young + spring = youth

Sample Sentences

지금 사춘기(思春期)인가 봐요.   = I guess they are in adolescence now.

 **moon / month**

Represents the shape of a crescent or half moon. When combined with other characters, it may take on other meanings, such as "meat 肉 [육]" or "boat 舟 [주]."

Character	Pronunciation	Meaning
月	월 [wol]	moon, month

 Stroke Order

Examples

월요일 wo-ryo-il	月曜日	moon + day of the week = Monday
월급 wol-geup	月給	month + give = monthly paycheck
매월 mae-wol	每月	every + month = every month, monthly
월초 wol-cho	月初	month + beginning = beginning of the month

Sample Sentences

월요일(月曜日)에는 항상 바빠요. = We are always busy on Mondays.

드디어 첫 월급(月給)을 받았어요. = I finally got my first monthly paycheck.

월초(月初)에 보는 거 어때요? = How about meeting in the beginning of the month?

명 **bright / next**

The sun (日) shines during the day and the moon (月) shines during the night. When you combine them, it represents brightness, or wishing for a bright future to come next.

Character	Pronunciation	Meaning
明	명 [myeong]	bright, next

✂ Breakdown

明	日	일	sun
明	月	월	moon

✏ Stroke Order

明 明 明 明 明 明 明 明

Examples

설명 seol-myeong	說明	say/talk + bright =	explanation
투명 tu-myeong	透明	transparent + bright =	transparent
분명 bun-myeong	分明	divide + bright =	clearly
현명 hyeon-myeong	賢明	wise + bright =	wisdom
증명 jeung-myeong	證明	evidence + bright =	proof
조명 jo-myeong	照明	shine + bright =	lighting
발명 bal-myeong	發明	bloom/develop + bright =	invention

Sample Sentences

제가 설명(說明)할게요.   = Let me explain.

시계가 분명(分明) 여기에 있었어요.   = There was definitely a clock here.

정말 현명(賢明)한 결정이네요.   = That's a very wise decision.

다 a lot of / many

🎵 Track 108

Pieces of meat (肉) are stacked together to mean many.

Character	Pronunciation	Meaning
多	다 [da]	a lot of, many

✂ Breakdown

多	夕→月→肉	육	meat
多	夕→月→肉	육	meat

Footnote
Ancient Chinese texts show "夕" is in fact meat, instead of a crescent moon.

✏ Stroke Order

Examples

다양 da-yang	多樣	a lot of + shape/form = various
다행 da-haeng	多幸	a lot of + lucky = lucky, fortunate
다정 da-jeong	多情	a lot of + meaning/love = kind, sweet
다수 da-su	多數	a lot of + numbers = many
다수결 da-su-gyeol	多數決	a lot of + numbers + decide = majority vote
다급 da-geup	多急	a lot of + urgent = urgent

Sample Sentences

정말 다행(多幸)이에요. = It's such a relief.

다수결(多數決)로 결정할까요? = Shall we decide by majority vote?

엄마가 다급(多急)하게 뛰어왔어요. = My mom ran over here urgently.

 전 front

Track 109

Represents the feet (止) of a man standing on the bow, or the front, of a ship (舟) sailing forward (刂) on the water.

Character	Pronunciation	Meaning
前	전 [jeon]	front, before

Breakdown

前	䒑 → 止	지	foot/stop
前	月 → 舟	주	boat
前	刂 = 刀	도	knife

Footnote
'Sword (刂)' is used in this character to symbolize a ship's bow cutting through the water as it sails forward.

Stroke Order

Examples

오전 o-jeon	午前	noon + before = morning
전반전 jeon-ban-jeon	前半戰	front + half + fight = first half of the game
전직 jeon-jik	前職	before + job = former occupation
여전 yeo-jeon	如前	same + before = same as before
전과 jeon-kkwa	前科	before + crime = criminal record

Sample Sentences

오전(午前)에 회의가 있어요.   = I have a meeting in the morning.

전반전(前半戰)이 벌써 끝났어요.   = The first half (of the game) is already over.

여전(如前)히 너무 예뻐요.   = (She is) still very pretty.

Review Quiz

1. Match the character to its sound!

   ㄱ. 日   a. 전
   ㄴ. 春   b. 다
   ㄷ. 前   c. 일
   ㄹ. 多   d. 명
   ㅁ. 明   e. 춘

2. What does this character mean?

   春   =   (   )

3. Find the character that is common among the following words and choose its English meaning.

   > 月曜日월요일   月給월급
   > 每月매월   月初월초

   a. morning   b. day   c. front   d. month

Answers: 1. ㄱ-c ㄴ-e ㄷ-a ㄹ-b ㅁ-d   2. spring   3. d

Flow Chart

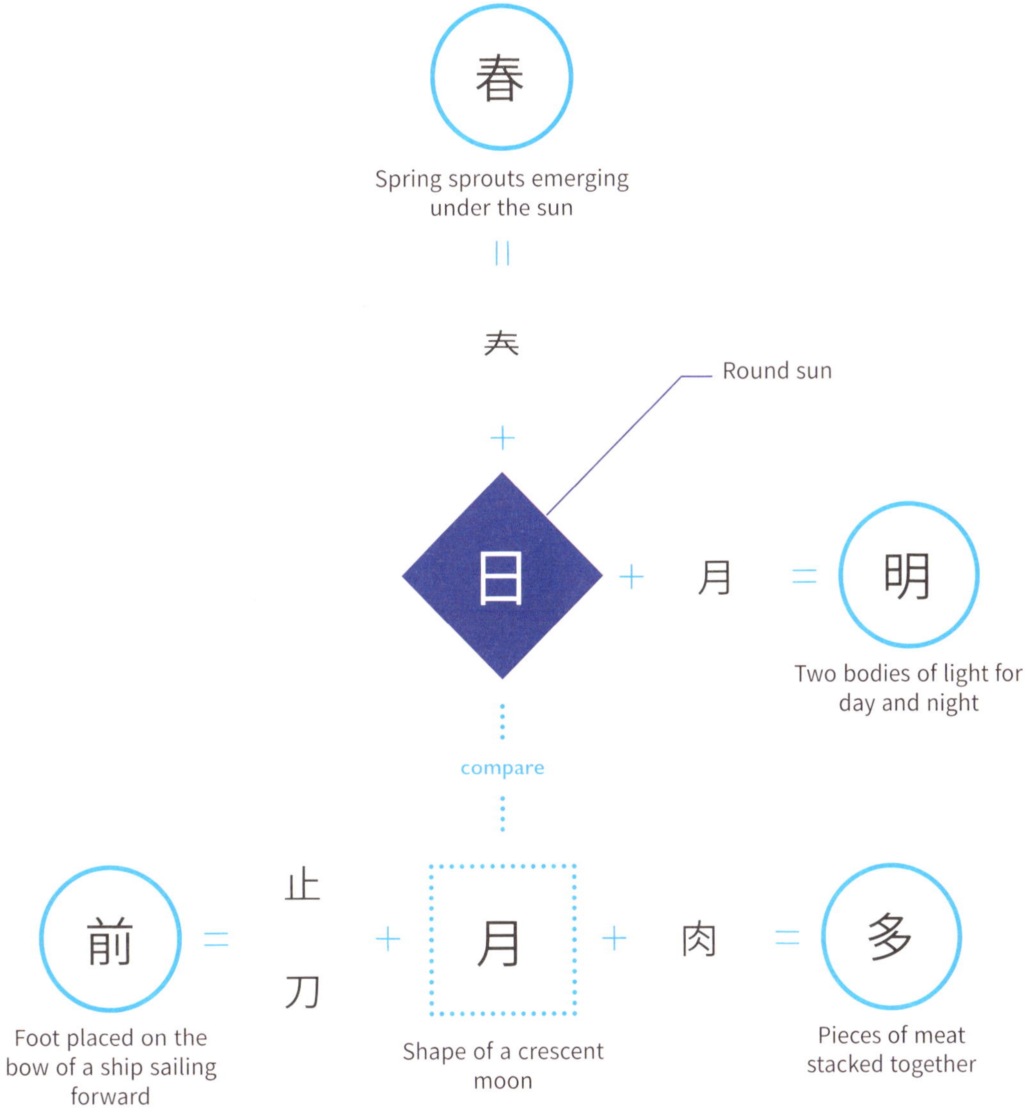

春

Spring sprouts emerging under the sun

=

夫

+

日 — Round sun

日 + 月 = 明

Two bodies of light for day and night

compare

前 = 止/刀 + 月 + 肉 = 多

Foot placed on the bow of a ship sailing forward

Shape of a crescent moon

Pieces of meat stacked together

 토 soil

 Track 110

Symbolizes a mound of earth or soil. Also represents a model of a male's genitals made from earth.

Character	Pronunciation	Meaning
土	토 [to]	soil, earth

 Stroke Order

Examples

토요일
to-yo-il

土曜日　　soil + day of the week = Saturday

Sample Sentences

오늘 토요일(土曜日)이에요.　　= Today is Saturday.

 지 land

 Track 111

Soil or land is where the food chain begins and is the basis of all life forms. This character is formed using soil (土), which most ground is made of, and a woman's genitals (也).

Character	Pronunciation	Meaning
地	지 [ji]	land, ground

Breakdown

地	土	토	soil
地	也	야	female genitals/also

Footnote
"也" - Represents the shape of a woman's genitals. When used on its own, it means 'also or too.'

Stroke Order

Examples

한글	漢字	뜻
지구 (ji-gu)	地球	land + ball = earth
지하 (ji-ha)	地下	ground + under = underground
지하철 (ji-ha-cheol)	地下鐵	ground + under + iron/track = subway
지진 (ji-jin)	地震	land + thunder/vibrate = earthquake
지방 (ji-bang)	地方	land + direction = area
번지 (beon-ji)	番地	order/number + land = house number
지옥 (ji-ok)	地獄	ground + prison = hell

Sample Sentences

지하(地下) 1층에 카페가 있어요.
= There is a café in the 1st basement level.

저는 매일 지하철(地下鐵)을 타요.
= I take the subway every day.

어제 지진(地震)이 났어요.
= There was an earthquake yesterday.

장 place

Track 112

A large area of land (土) with sunlight shining upon it (昜) provides a suitable place for people to gather and hold events.

Character	Pronunciation	Meaning
場	장 [jang]	place

Breakdown

| 場 | 土 | 토 | soil |
| 場 | 昜 | 양 | sun |

Footnote
"昜" - At dawn (旦), the edge of the rising sun burns in a haze (勿).

Stroke Order

場 場 場 場 場 場 場 場 場 場 場 場

Examples

공장
gong-jang

工場   make + place = factory

장소 jang-so	場所	place + place = place
당장 dang-jang	當場	this/that + place/time = right now
광장 gwang-jang	廣場	large + place = plaza
직장 jik-jang	職場	duty/job + place = work, workplace
직장인 jik-jang-in	職場人	workplace + person = company employee
극장 geuk-jang	劇場	play + place = theater
주차장 ju-cha-jang	駐車場	stay + car + place = parking lot
수영장 su-yeong-jang	水泳場	swim + place = swimming pool
입장 ip-jang	入場	enter + place = entrance
퇴장 toe-jang	退場	step back + place = exit
입장료 ip-jang-ryo	入場料	enter + place + count/fee = entrance fee

Sample Sentences

당장(當場) 거기서 나오세요. = Get out of there right now.

주말에 극장(劇場)에 갈 거예요. = I will go to the theater over the weekend.

주차장(駐車場)이 어디예요? = Where is the parking lot?

Review Quiz

1. Match the character to its sound!

   ㄱ. 場   a. 장

   ㄴ. 土   b. 토

2. What does this character mean?

   土   =   (   )

3. Find the character that is common among the following words and choose its English meaning.

   地震지진   地球지구
   地下지하   地下鐵지하철

   a. earthquake   b. be born / life   c. land   d. place

Answers: 1. ㄱ - a ㄴ - b   2. soil   3. c

Flow Chart

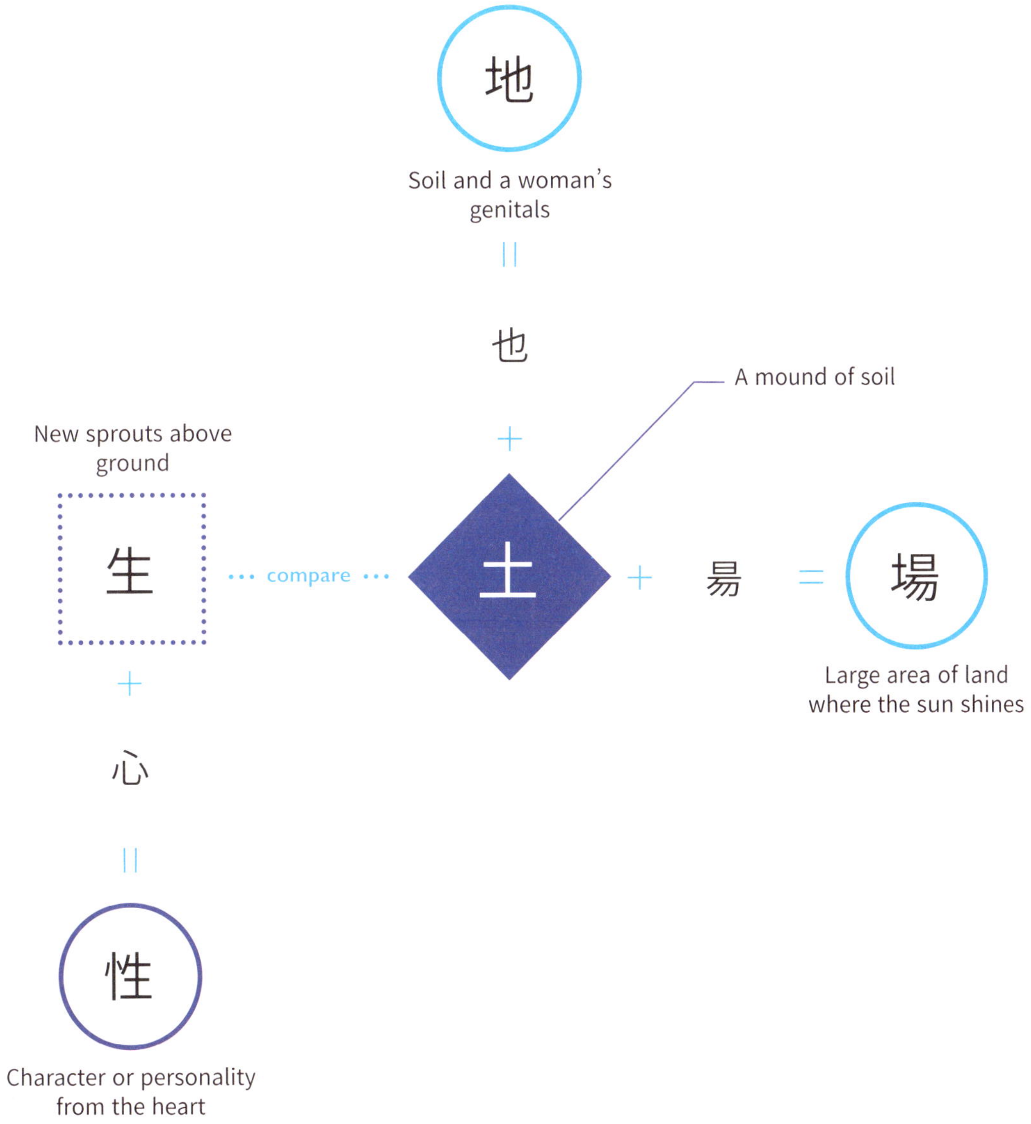

地

Soil and a woman's genitals

=

也

+

土 — A mound of soil

生 New sprouts above ground

··· compare ···

土 + 昜 = 場

Large area of land where the sun shines

+

心

=

性

Character or personality from the heart

Miscellaneous

小一事一水一酒一上一下一

 소 **small**

🎵 Track 113

Signifies a group of three small dots (丶).

Character	Pronunciation	Meaning
小	소 [so]	small

✏️ Stroke Order

Examples

소포 so-po	小包	small + wrap =	parcel
소심 so-sim	小心	small + mind =	timid
소설 so-seol	小說	small + word/narrate =	novel
최소 choe-so	最小	most + small =	smallest, minimum
축소 chuk-sso	縮小	reduce + small =	reduction

Sample Sentences

소포(小包)가 왔어요. = A parcel came.

저는 소설(小說)책을 좋아해요. = I like novels.

파티에 최소(最小) 100명은 올 거예요. = A minimum of 100 people will come to the party.

 work

 Track 114

In an agricultural society, it was common to work with hand-held (ヨ) farming tools (中), like rakes or spades.

Character	Pronunciation	Meaning
事	사 [sa]	work, business, occasion, affair

✂ Breakdown

事	中	symbol	farming tools
事	ヨ	계	hand

✏ Stroke Order

事 事 事 事 事 事 事 事

Examples

식사 sik-ssa	食事	meal + work = have a meal
사실 sa-sil	事實	occasion + truly = fact
사업 sa-eop	事業	work/business + business/company = business
사건 sa-kkeon	事件	affair + affair = incident, affair
사례 sa-rye	事例	occasion + example = example, case
행사 haeng-sa	行事	go + occasion = event
인사 in-sa	人事	person + work = greeting
농사 nong-sa	農事	farming + work = farming
사연 sa-yeon	事緣	occasion + reason = story
사무실 sa-mu-sil	事務室	work + work + room = office

Sample Sentences

사실(事實) 그거 제가 했어요. = In fact, I did it.

행사(行事) 어디에서 해요? = Where does the event take place?

제 사무실(事務室)에서 만날까요? = Shall we meet in my office?

Learn Essential Chinese Characters Used in the Korean Language

 水 수 **water**

 Track 115

Symbolizes water flowing down a river (水).

Character	Pronunciation	Meaning
水	수 [su]	water

✏️ Stroke Order

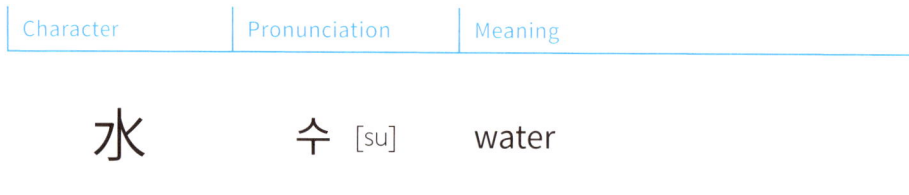

Examples

수영 su-yeong	水泳	water + swim = swimming
생수 saeng-su	生水	fresh + water = mineral water
음료수 eum-nyo-su	飲料水	drink + ingredient + water = beverage
온수 on-su	溫水	warm + water = hot water, warm water
냉수 naeng-su	冷水	cold + water = cold water
수준 su-jun	水準	water + standard = level, standard
홍수 hong-su	洪水	large + water = flood

Sample Sentences

제 꿈은 수영(水泳) 선수예요. = My dream is to become a swimmer.

생수(生水) 주세요. = Please give me mineral water.

이 반은 수준(水準)이 너무 높아요. = The level of this class is too high.

 **주** **alcoholic drinks**

 Track 116

An empty bottle (酉) is filled with wine (or alcohol in general) in the form of liquid (氵).

Character	Pronunciation	Meaning
酒	주 [ju]	alcohol

✂ **Breakdown**

酒	氵 = 水	수	water
酒	酉	유	empty bottle

Footnote

"酉" - This character is derived from the shape of a traditional vessel that held wine.

✏ **Stroke Order**

Examples

맥주 maek-jju	麥酒	barley + alcohol = beer
생맥주 saeng-maek-jju	生麥酒	fresh + barley + alcohol = draft beer
양주 yang-ju	洋酒	the West + alcohol = liquor, western-style alcohol (such as vodka or rum)
음주 eum-ju	飮酒	drink + alcohol = drinking

Sample Sentences

생맥주(生麥酒) 한 잔 주세요. = Give me a pint of draft beer.

양주(洋酒)는 너무 독해요. = Liquor is too strong.

음주(飮酒)운전 하지 마세요. = Don't drink and drive.

Review Quiz

1. Match the character to its sound!

ㄱ. 酒   a. 사

ㄴ. 小   b. 주

ㄷ. 事   c. 소

2. What does this character mean?

酒 = (   )

3. Find the character that is common among the following words and choose its English meaning.

水泳수영   溫水온수
冷水냉수   洪水홍수

a. swimming   b. water   c. flood   d. sea

Answers: 1. ㄱ - b ㄴ - c ㄷ - a   2. alcoholic drinks   3. b

Flow Chart

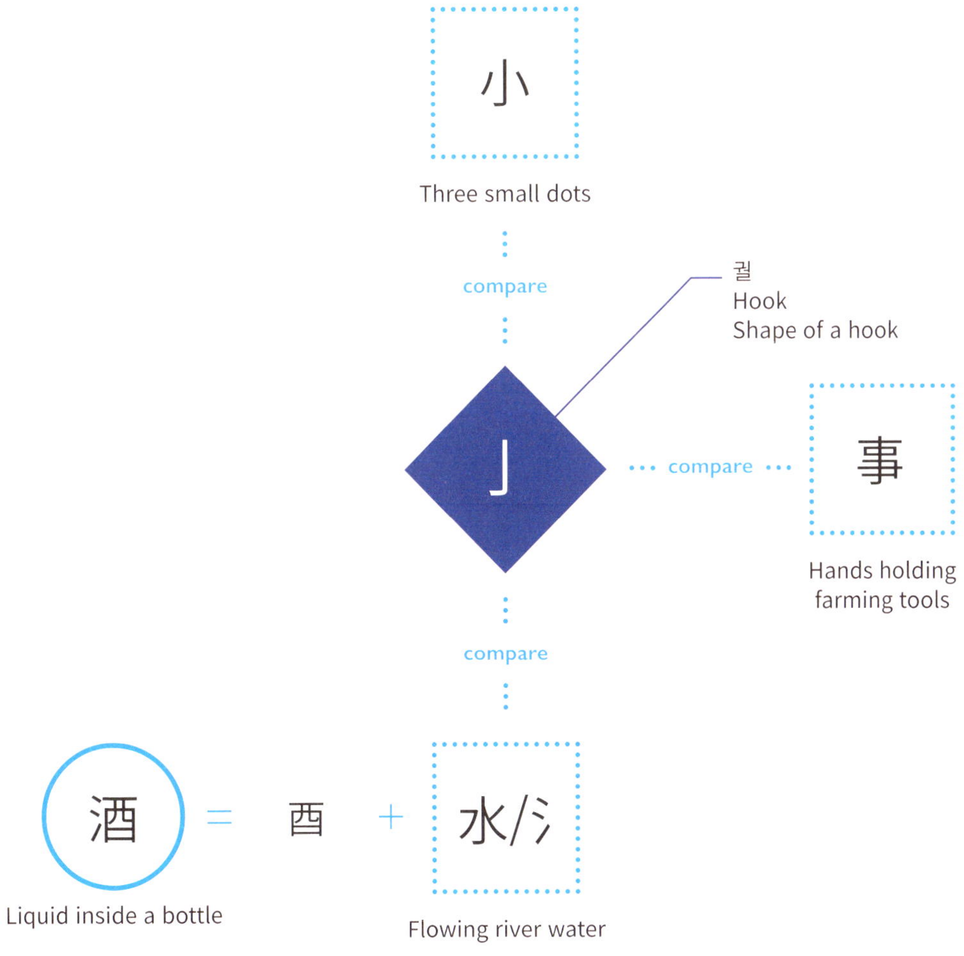

小
Three small dots

compare

궐
Hook
Shape of a hook

亅

compare ··· 事

Hands holding farming tools

compare

酒 = 酉 + 水/氵

Liquid inside a bottle

Flowing river water

Learn Essential Chinese Characters Used in the Korean Language

 상 up

Track 117

A symbol (卜) above a line that represents the base (一).

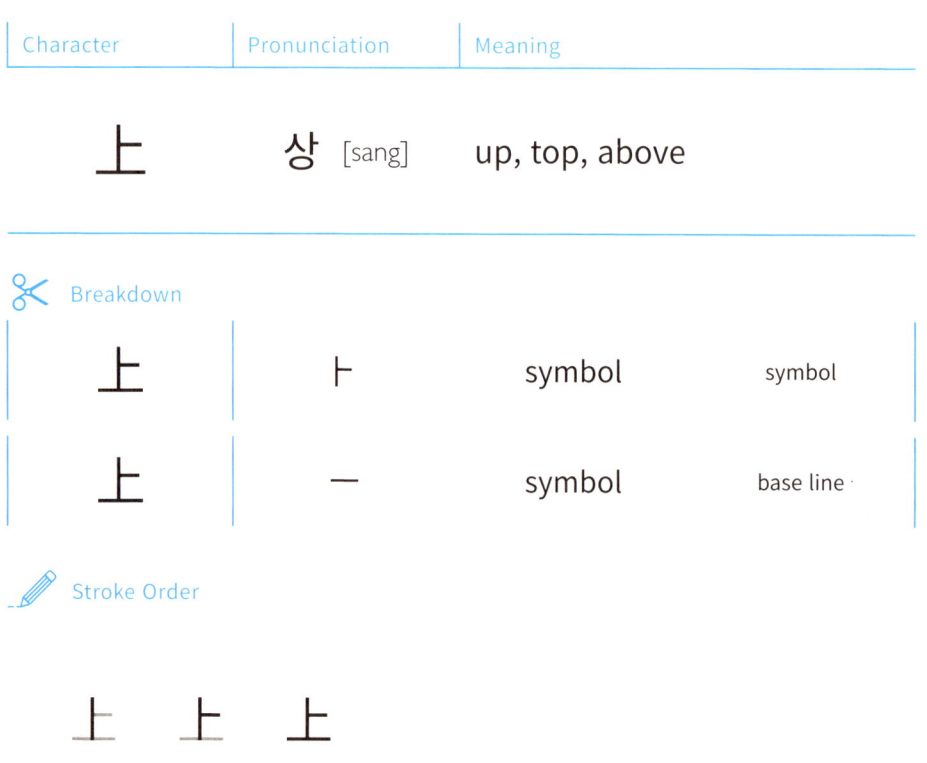

Examples

옥상 ok-ssang	屋上	house + top = rooftop
정상 jeong-sang	頂上	top of one's head + top = summit, top
인상 in-sang	引上	pull + up = raise, increase
상사 sang-sa	上司	top/up + undertake = superior

Sample Sentences

옥상(屋上)에 빨래를 널었어요. = I hung the laundry out on the rooftop.

월급이 인상(引上)됐어요. = My pay has been raised.

직장 상사(上司) 때문에 너무 힘들어요. = I am so stressed out because of my boss at work.

 하 down

 Track 118

A symbol (卜) below a line that represents the base (一).

Character	Pronunciation	Meaning
下	하 [ha]	down, bottom, below

✂ Breakdown

下	一	symbol	base line
下	卜	symbol	symbol

✏ Stroke Order

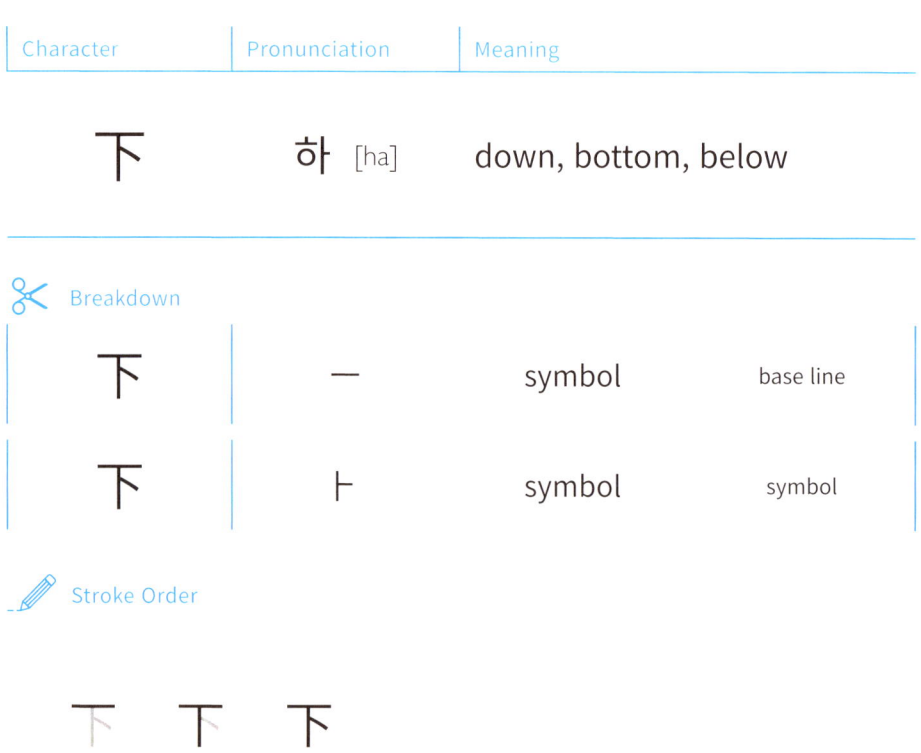

Examples

| 지하
ji-ha	地下	ground + under = underground
인하
i-na	引下	pull + down = reduction
낙하산
na-ka-san	落下傘	fall + down + umbrella = parachute

Sample Sentences

저 지금 지하(地下) 1층에 있어요. = I am now in the 1st basement level.

가격이 인하(引下)되었어요. = The price has been reduced.

낙하산(落下傘)이 안 펴져요. = The parachute won't open.

Review Quiz

1. Match the character to its sound!

ㄱ. 上				a. 하

ㄴ. 下				b. 상

2. What does this character mean?

下　=　(　　　　　　)

3. Find the character that is common among the following words and choose its English meaning.

| 屋上옥상　　頂上정상　　引上인상　　上司상사 |

a. rooftop   b. underground   c. superior   d. up

Answers: 1. ㄱ - b ㄴ - a   2. down   3. d

Flow Chart

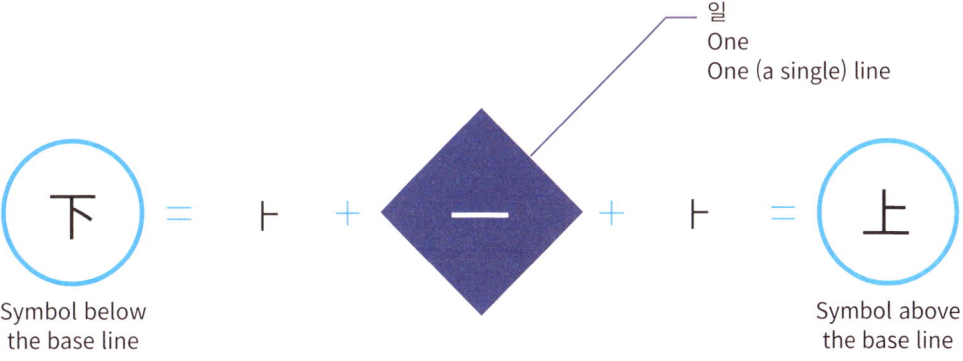

일
One
One (a single) line

Symbol below the base line

Symbol above the base line

Hanja Board Game

1. Each team prepares 2 dice and 2 horses.

2. Throw 2 dice at the same time and subtract the number of one dice from the other. For example, you move 3 spots if the numbers are 5 and 2, and you stay at the same spot if the numbers are both 6.

3. Say the Chinese character of the spot that you land on. If you don't remember, go back to your last spot.

4. If you arrive at the spot your opponent's horse is at, you have caught the horse. The caught horse goes back to "start," and the team who caught the horse throws the dice again. If both of your horses are on the same spot, then only one goes back to "start."

5. If you land on a spot with an arrow, you must follow that arrow on your next turn. The pink arrows jump backward to the character's antonym, and the blue arrows jump forward to the character's synonym.

6. You can move both of your horses at the same time.

7. Follow the path. Rest if you arrive at "Rest (한 번 쉬기)," go back to start if you land on "Lose (꽝)," or move forward (앞으로) or backward (뒤로) the indicated number of spaces.

8. The first team to have both horses cross the finish line wins!

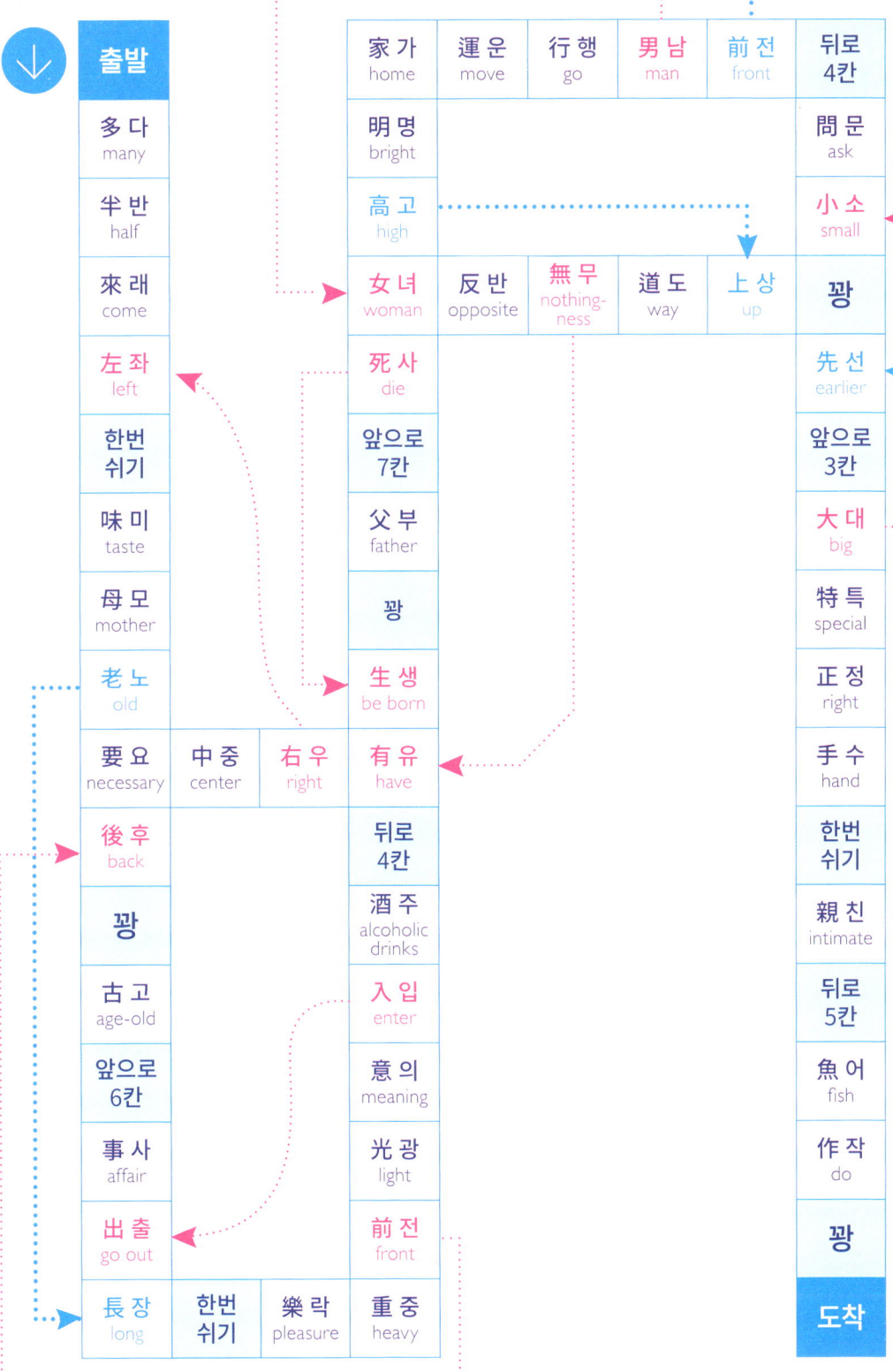

Index

ㄱ

가구 furniture	185	
가난 poverty	185	
가명 alias, pseudonym	95	
가속 acceleration	99	
가수 singer	132, 133	
가입 join	99	
가장 head of the family, breadwinner	47, 185	
가족 family	185	
가출 running away from home	157	
각자 each, respectively	79	
간격 interval, space	197	
간식 snack	233	
갈색 brown	33	
감동 touched, touching	229	
감성 sensibility	121	
감정 emotion	125	
강남 Gangnam, district south of the Han River	203	
강요 pressure, coercion	63	
강점 strength, strong point	221	
개성 individuality	121	
개인 individual	17	
거래 deal, transaction	271	
결과 result	113	
결론 conclusion	113	
결말 ending	113	
결심 decision	117	
결혼 marriage	113	
결혼식 wedding	113	
경품 prize, giveaway prize	97	
고가 high price	109	
고대 ancient	107	
고등학교 high school	55	
고령 old age	109	
고모 father's sister, aunt	65	
고물 junk	107	
고속 도로 expressway	109	

고액 large amount of money	109	관광 sightseeing	31
고유 inherent, characteristic	147	관광지 tourist spot	31
고의 on purpose, intention	89	관심 interest	117
고전 classic	107	광장 plaza	309
고참 senior	107	교과서 textbook	57
고혈압 hypertension, high blood pressure	109	교대 rotation, taking turns, shift	23
공개 make public	249	교복 school uniform	269
공공 public	249	교사 teacher	57
공무원 civil servant	249	교수 professor	57
공식 formula, formal	249	교실 classroom	57, 189
공약 pledge	249	교육 education	57
공연 performance, show	249	교장 principal, headmaster	47, 269
공원 park	249	교통 traffic	179
공유 share	147	구급차 ambulance	265
공장 factory	308	국가 nation, country	101, 185
공통점 common ground	179	국내 domestic	101, 201
공휴일 public holiday	249, 291	국민 nation, people, the public	103
과식 overeating	233	국사 national history	101
과자 snacks	53	국제 international	101

국화 national flower	41	남매 brother and sister	227
국회 National Assembly	101, 235	남자 man	53, 227
귀중 precious	263	남편 husband	227
극장 theater	309	남학생 male student	227
금요일 Friday	237	남해 South Sea	203
급행 rush	173	내년 next year	25, 271
기간 period, term	197	내용 content	201
기념품 souvenir	97	내일 tomorrow	271, 290, 291
기억력 memory	225	냉수 cold water	319
기운 energy, stamina	175	노동 labor	229
기차 train	264, 265	노력 effort	225
기특 commendable, praiseworthy	139	노부부 old couple	45
기회 opportunity	235	노안 presbyopia, age-related farsightedness	45

ㄴ

		노약자 the old and the infirm	45
낙천적 optimistic	273	노인 elderly, old person	17, 45
낙하산 parachute	327	노인정 senior citizens' center	45
난민 refugee	103	노처녀 old unmarried woman, "old maid"	45
남녀 man and woman	227	노총각 old bachelor	45

335

노후 one's later years	45
녹색 green	33
녹차 green tea	283
농사 farming	317
누명 false charge	95
능력 ability	225

ㄷ

다과 refreshments	283
다급 urgent	299
다수 many	299
다수결 majority vote	299
다양 various	299
다정 kindness, kind-heartedness	125, 299
다행 lucky, fortunate	299
단점 shortcoming	221
당분간 for a while	247
당시 at that time	137
당일 the very day	291

당장 right now	309
대기업 major company	73
대리 deputy	23
대부분 most	247
대신 instead	23, 71
대역 understudy, stand-in	23
대장 group leader, leader of the pack	47
대중 public	73
대통령 president	73
대표 representative	23
대학 university	73
대학교 university	55
대회 convention, conference, competition, championship	73, 235
도덕 morality, ethics	177
도로 road	177
도시 city	205
독신 unmarried person, single	71
독특 unique	139

동기 motive	229
동물 animal	229
동물원 zoo	229
동복 winter clothing (usually in school)	169
동생 younger brother or sister	285
동양 the Orient, the East	259
동점 tie	221
동정 sympathy	125
동해 the East Sea	259
동호회 club, society	61
등교 go to school	269
등산 hiking	279

ㅁ

마녀 witch	59
마차 carriage	265
만족 satisfaction	155
망신 shame	71
매년 every year	25
매력 charm	225
매월 every month, monthly	295
매일 every day, daily	290, 291
맥주 beer	321
면회 visit (someone at a hospital/prison/army)	235
명문 prestigious	95
명예 honor	95
명작 masterpiece	21
명절 (national) holiday	95
명품 masterpiece, brand-name product	95
모교 alma mater	65, 269
모국어 mother tongue	65
모녀 mother and daughter	65
모음 vowel	65
모자 mother and son	65
목마 wooden horse	257
목요일 Thursday	257

목재 lumber	257	문화 culture	39, 77
무료 free of charge	219	미각 palate, taste	275
무사 safe	219	미남 good-looking man, handsome man	75, 227
무선 wireless	219	미녀 beautiful woman	59
무시 disregard	219	미래 future	271
무의미 meaningless	275	미술 art, fine art	75
무작정 blindly, thoughtlessly	219	미식가 gourmet	75
무조건 unconditional	219	미용실 beauty salon	75
무죄 innocence	219	미인 beautiful woman	75
무지 ignorance	219	민간인 civilian	103
무효 invalidity, invalid	219	민박 bed and breakfast (accommodation)	103
문맹 illiteracy	77	민속 folklore	103
문법 grammar	77	민원 civil complaint	103
문병 visiting a sick person	195		
문의 inquire	195		

ㅂ

문자 letter	77	박수 clapping	133
문장 sentence	77	반대 opposition, objection	149
문제 question, problem	161, 195	반복 repetition	149
문학 literature	77		

반사 reflection	149	부고 a notice of death	107
반성 repent, self-remorse	149	부녀 father and daughter	135
반세기 half a century	245	부동산 real estate	229
반숙 soft-boiled	245	부모 parents	135
반응 reaction	149	부분 part	247
반전 reversal, plot twist	149	부인 wife	17
반지 ring	245	부자 father and son	135
반칙 foul, rule violation, cheating	149	부족 shortage	155
반항 defiance	149	북극 the North Pole	43
발명 invention	297	분명 clearly	247, 297
방문 visit	195	분석 analysis	247
방학 vacation	55	분식 flour-based food	233
번지 house number	307	분야 area, field	247
벌금 fine, penalty	237	불만족 dissatisfaction	155
변신 transformation	71	불안 anxiety	187
변화 change	39	비상구 emergency exit	93
보통 normal	179	비행기 airplane	173
복고 retro	107		
복도 corridor	177		

ㅅ

사건 incident, affair	317
사례 example, case	317
사망 death	49
사망률 death rate	49
사망자 the dead, dead person	49
사무실 office	189, 317
사별 separation by death	49
사실 fact	317
사업 business	317
사연 story	317
사장 president, CEO	47
사정 reason, circumstances	125
사진 picture	251
사춘기 adolescence, puberty	293
사형 death penalty	49
사회 society	235
상반기 the first half of the year	245
상사 superior	325
색맹 color-blindness	33

색연필 colored pencil	33
생맥주 draft beer	321
생명 life	285
생산 production	285
생선 fish	285
생수 mineral water	285, 319
생일 birthday	285, 290, 291
생화 natural flower, real flower	41
서명 signature	95
서양 the West	261
서해 the West Sea, the Yellow Sea	261
선배 older alumnus, more experienced person in the group	29
선불 payment in advance, prepayment	29
선생 teacher	29, 285
선수 player	132
선약 previous engagement	29
선진국 advanced country	29
선착순 first come, first served	29

선호 preference	61		소중 precious	263
설명 explanation	297		소통 communication	179
성격 personality	121		소포 parcel	315
성별 gender	121		소화 digestion	39
성분 ingredient	247		소화기 fire extinguisher	215
성의 sincerity, sincere effort	89		손자 grandson	53
성장 growth	47		송금 wire, transfer	237
성품 personality, character	97		수건 towel	133
세계 world	281		수분 moisture	247
세계 지도 world map	281		수수료 commision, fee	133
세계사 world history	281		수술 surgery	133
세금 tax	237		수영 swimming	319
세대 generation	23, 281		수영장 swimming pool	309
세상 world, society	281		수요 demand	63
세차 car wash	265		수입 income	19
소녀 girl	59		수정 modification	159
소년 boy	25		수제 handmade, handcrafted	133
소설 novel	315		수준 level, standard	319
소심 timid	315		수첩 notebook	132

수표 check	133	식품 food	97
숙제 homework	161	신년 new year	25
순간 moment	197	신랑 groom	87
순진 naive	251	신문 newspaper	87
시간 time	137, 197	신부(新婦) bride	87
시간표 timetable	137	신부(神父) priest	135
시계 clock, watch	137	신분 position, status	71
시내 downtown	201	신생아 newborn baby	87
시대 historical period, era	23, 137	신인 rookie	87
시민 citizen	205	신입 newcomer, new member	87
시작 start	21	신입생 freshman	19, 87
시장 market	205	신제품 new product	87
시청 city hall	205	신중 caution	263
식구 family member	93, 233	신학기 new semester	87
식당 restaurant	233	실내 indoor	189
식목일 Arbor Day	257	실명 autonym, real name	95
식사 have a meal	232, 233, 317	실수 mistake	132, 133
식욕 appetite	233	실외 outdoor	189
식탁 dinner table	232	심장 heart	116

십대 teenage years	23	

ㅇ

악기 musical instrument	273	
악보 music score, sheet music	273	
악수 handshake	133	
악어 crocodile, alligator	35	
안내 guide	201	
안부 inquire about someone, ask whether someone is well or not	187	
안전 safe	187	
안정 stability	187	
애완동물 pet	123	
애인 lover (boyfriend, girlfriend)	123	
애정 affection	123	
액자 frame	53	
야간 night, the night time	197	
야광 glow-in-the-dark, luminous	31	
야생 wild	285	

약점 weakness	221
양주 liquor, western-style alcohol (such as vodka or rum)	321
양호 satisfactory, fine	61
어류 fish, various kinds of fish	35
여왕 queen	59
여자 woman	53, 59
여전 same as before	301
여학생 female student	59
여행 travel	173
여행사 travel agency	173
연결 connection	113
연말 the end of the year	25
연애 dating, seeing someone	123
연하 being younger than someone	25
열대어 tropical fish	35
열심 diligent	117
열정 passion	125
염색 dyeing	33
영광 glory, honor	31

예문 sample sentence	77	우산 umbrella	207
오락 entertainment, game	273	우선 above all	29
오락실 (video) arcade	273	우유 milk	243
오전 morning	301	우정 friendship	125
오후 afternoon	167	우측 the right side, one's right	143
옥상 rooftop	325	우회전 right turn	143
온수 hot water, warm water	319	운동 exercise	175
왕자 prince	53	운동장 schoolyard	175
외국 foreign country	101	운명 fate	175
외국어 foreign language	101	운세 fortune	175
외국인 foreigner	17, 101	운전 drive	175
외식 eating out	233	운전면허 driver's license	175
외출 going out, outing	157	운행 running/operating a vehicle	173
요금 charge, fee	237	원래 original, originally	271
요령 trick, know-how	63	원점 starting point	221
요약 sum up	63	월급 monthly paycheck	295
요청 request	63	월요일 Monday	295
욕심 greed	117	월초 beginning of the month	295
우비 raincoat	207	유래 origin	271

유명 famous	95, 147		이성 reason, rational thinking	121
유모차 stroller	65, 265		이자 interest	53
유죄 guilty	147		익명 anonymous	95
유학 studying abroad	55		인간 human	17, 197
유행 trend	173		인구 population	17, 93
은행 bank	173		인기 popularity	17
음료수 beverage	319		인물 person	17
음식 food	232		인사 greeting	17, 317
음식점 restaurant	232		인상 raise, increase	325
음악 music	273		인어 mermaid	35
음주 drinking	321		인하 reduction	327
의견 opinion	89		일기 diary	290, 291
의미 meaning	89, 275		일몰 sunset	291
의심 doubt	116, 117		일상 everyday life	291
의자 chair	53		일주일 a week, one week	291
의지 will	89		일출 sunrise	291
이동 movement (to a different location)	229		임시 temporary	137
이모 mother's sister, aunt	65		입구 entrance	19, 93
이민 emigration	103		입금 deposit	19

입문 introduction (to a field of study)	193		자존심 self-esteem	79, 117
입사 joining a company	19		작가 author	21, 185
입양 adoption	19		작곡 music composition, writing music	21
입원 being hospitalized	19		작년 last year	25
입장 entrance	309		작동 (machine) operation, working, running	229
입장료 entrance fee, admission	19, 309		작문 composition	21
입학 entering school, starting school	19, 55		작사 writing lyrics	21
			작업 work	21
			작품 work (of art)	21, 97
			잠시 short while	137
			장관 minister	47
자녀 children	59		장남 the oldest son	47, 227
자동차 car	79, 264, 265		장래 future	271
자살 suicide	79		장소 place	309
자식 offspring	53		장수 longevity	47
자신 oneself	71		장점 advantage, strength	47, 221
자신감 self-confidence	79		장학금 scholarship	237
자연 nature	79		저금 saving	237
자유 freedom	79		전과 criminal record	301
자전거 bicycle	79, 265			

ㅈ

전국 the whole country	101		제자 student	53
전문가 expert	185		제작 making, production	21
전반 the first half	245		제품 product	97
전반전 first half of the game	301		조명 lighting	297
전신 whole body	71		조미료 seasoning	275
전직 former occupation	301		조식 breakfast	233
절반 half	245		조심 be careful	117
점선 dotted line	221		조작 fabrication	21
점수 score, point	221		존중 respect	263
정거장 station	265		종교 religion	57
정답 correct answer	159		좌측 the left side, one's left	145
정문 front door	193		좌회전 left turn	145
정보 information	125		주문 order	77
정상(正常) normal	159		주의 caution, attention	89
정상(頂上) summit, top	325		주인 owner	17
정중 polite	263		주인공 hero, heroine	249
정직 honesty	159		주제 subject, topic	161
정확 accurate	159		주차장 parking lot	264, 265, 309
제목 title	161		중간 middle	111, 197

중년 middle age	25		진실 truth	251
중단 halt, stop	111		진심 sincere, sincerity	117, 251
중독 addiction	111		진지 serious	251
중복 repetition	263		진품 genuine article, authentic object	251
중심 center	111, 116		질문 question	195
중요 important	63, 263		집중 concentration	111
중학교 middle school	55			
즉시 immediately	137			

大

증가 increase	99		차선 traffic lane	264
증명 proof	297		차세대 next generation	281
지구 earth	307		참가 participation	99
지명 place name	95		창구 counter	93
지방 area	307		창문 window	193
지옥 hell	307		채식 vegetarian diet	233
지진 earthquake	307		채점 marking	221
지하 underground	307		처녀 single woman	59
지하철 subway	307		천국 heaven	101
직장 work, workplace	309		청춘 youth	293
직장인 company employee	309		체력 physical strength, stamina	225

체중 bodyweight	263
초등학교 elementary school	55
최고 the best	109
최대 most, biggest	73
최소 smallest, minimum	315
최신 the newest, the latest	87
추가 addition	99
추석 Chuseok, Korean harvest festival	217
추수 harvest	217
축소 reduction	315
출구 exit	93, 157
출근 going to work	157
출발 departure	157
출석 attendance	157
출세 success	281
출시 launch, hit the market	205
출신 origin	71, 157
출입 going in and out	19
출입문 gate	157

출장 business trip	157
충동 impulse	229
충분 enough	247
충족 satisfy	155
취미 hobby	275
친구 friend	85
친절 kind	85
친척 relative	85
친필 handwriting	85
친환경 environmentally-friendly	85

ㅌ

탈출 escape	157
토요일 Saturday	305
통과 pass	179
통역 translation, interpretation	179
통장 bankbook	179
통화 phone call	179
퇴장 exit	309

투명 transparent	297
특강 special lecture	139
특권 privilege	139
특기 specialty	139
특별 special	139
특집 special edition, special episode	139
특징 characteristic, feature	139

ㅍ

패배 defeat	43
편안 comfortable	187
평생 lifetime	285
표정 facial expression	125
품질 quality	97
풍족 affluence	155
필독 required reading, must-read	119
필수 mandatory, compulsory	119
필요 need	63, 119

ㅎ

하반기 the second half of the year	245
하복 summer clothing (usually in school)	165
하필 why on earth, of all occasions	119
학교 school	55, 269
학년 grade	25, 55
학력 academic ability, academic background	225
학문 study	195
학부모 student's parent	65
학생 student	55, 285
한심 pathetic	117
합의 agreement	89
항구 harbor	93
핵심 core	117
행동 act, action	173, 229
행사 event	173, 317
행운 good luck	175

향신료 spice	83
허무 futility	219
현금 cash	237
현명 wisdom	297
협력 collaboration	225
호감 having a good feeling, likeable	61
홍수 flood	319
홍차 black tea	283
화가 painter	185
화단 flower bed	41
화분 flowerpot	41
화산 volcano	215, 279
화상 burn, scald	215
화성 Mars	215
화요일 Tuesday	215
화장 makeup	39
화장실 bathroom, toilet	39, 189
화장품 cosmetics	39, 97
화재 fire, blaze	215

화학 chemistry	39
확대 expansion, enlargement	73
활동 activity	229
회계 accounting	235
회사 company	235
회식 company dinner	233
회원 member	235
회의 conference	235
회의실 conference room	189
회장 chairman, president	47, 235
효녀 filial daughter	59
효도 filial piety	177
후광 halo	31
후문 back gate, rumor	167, 193
후반 the second half	245
후배 junior	167
후원 sponsorship	167
후원금 donation	167
후원자 sponsor	167

후유증 aftermath	167
후진 reversing, backing up (the car)	167
후회 regret	167
휴게실 lounge	189
휴일 day off, holiday	291